Genius Recipe for

Luscious Ice Creams without a Machine

... or much time or effort or having to mash the stuff as it freezes

Suzy Bowler

Copyright 2014 Suzy Bowler

All Rights Reserved

This book or any portion thereof may not be reproduced or used in any manner whatsoever without the express permission of the publisher except for the use of brief quotations in a book review.

ISBN-13: 978-1514380628

ISBN-10: 1514380625

About the Author

After 14 years running her own restaurants and hotel in Cornwall (in partnership with her sister Maggie Weaver) Suzy Bowler started travelling; cooked in a ski resort in the French Alps, on a passage making yacht around Madeira and the Canary Islands, in New Zealand and on a catamaran in the Caribbean before making her home in the British Virgin Islands where she worked as a chef for many years.

Having learned so very much about food and cooking she returned to Cornwall to spend her dotage passing it on (or "sitting on the settee" as her partner calls it!)

suddenlunch.blogspot.co.uk

Also by Suzy Bowler

The Genius Recipes Series

Sorbets & Granitas

SOUP (almost) the Only Recipe You'll Ever Need

The Secret Life of Scones: There's so very much more to this simple recipe than perhaps you realise!

Other Books and eBooks

Creative Ways to Use Up Leftovers: An Inspiring A – Z of Ingredients and Delicious Ideas

Easy Festive Food for a Stress-Free Christmas

Food for Love: Eat your Way to a Better Sex Life ~ Win/Win Situation!

500+ Truly Useful Cooking Tips & Techniques: No Silly Hacks!

Easy Ways to Pimp your Food

See all Suzy's books here –
amazon.co.uk/Suzy-Bowler/e/B00AG1YUKE/

Genius Recipes

It seems recently that the words "genius recipe" are applied to many different dishes some of which are very good indeed but for me the thing that really makes a recipe "genius" is flexibility. If you understand the principles; the why and how a recipe works, you can add to it, vary it and create brilliant dishes of your very own.

In these pages I give more than 100 great ice creams using one simple "genius" recipe together with another 35 or so recipes and instructions for ancillaries and inclusions such as how to make caramel, a failproof meringue recipe and lots of delicious syrups and sauces. I give lots of serving and presentation suggestions and also go into detail as to why and how this method works so well and ways you can confidently vary it to make your own unique ice creams.

This is the first in series of books I am writing on different Genius Recipes – the second is just a booklet really, a companion volume to this book concerning sorbets and granitas which, whilst not requiring an ice cream machine are based on a different genius recipe. Number three is a very useful way of making soup with recipes from leek and potato to Caribbean Callaloo, and number four is about a wonderfully flexible scone recipe that can also be used to also make doughnuts, dumplings, biscuits, griddle cakes, shortcakes, rock cakes, crumbles, cobbles, pie crusts and slumps.

In each case I give the one key "genius" recipe together with lots of recipes and all the information and help you need to invent your own creations. I have two more on the fire (about a superb way of cooking onions and very useful muffin recipe, but not at the same time).

With some of these in your brain, or other handy place, then you are really ready to cook!

~ Contents ~

Intro, Info and Genius Recipe ~ 1

American Alternatives to English Ingredients * The Genius Recipe *
Clotted Cream Variation * Folding In * Marbling *
Dulce de Leche * Adding Inclusions * Freezing & Shelf Life *
Sphenopalatine Ganglioneuralgia!

Very, Very Easy Ice Creams ~ 9

Maple Syrup Ice Cream * 5 Honey Ice Creams * Thunder & Lightening
Dulce de Leche Ripple * Crunchy Peanut Butter Ice Cream
Peanut Butter & Chocolate Swirl * P. B. & J. I. C * Marmalade or Jam Ice Creams
Lemon (Orange, Lime or Raspberry) Curd Ice Cream
Brandied Mincemeat Ice Cream * Toffee Ripple * Nutella Fudge Ripple
Elderflower * Syrup Ice Creams in general * Coffee Ice Cream

Slightly More Complicated ~ 18

Double Vanilla * Island Spice * Liquorice & Salted Liquorice * Lemon Posset Ice Cream
Lemon Meringue * St. Clements * Cocoa Nib Crunch * Caramel Ice Cream *
Caramelised Cinnamon * Salted Caramel Crunch * Brown Sugar

Fruits ~ 26

Simple Strawberry * Raspberry Ripple * Iced Blueberry Fool
Papaya & Ginger * Peaches 'n' Cream * Peach Melba * Wild Blackberry * Rhubarb
Mango-Lime * Sautéed Peach and Brown Sugar Ice Cream * Toffee Apple * Burnt Orange
Port & Orange * Rum Roasted Banana * Banana Fudge
Honey Roasted Fig * Butterscotch Baked Pear * Slow Roasted Pineapple

Nuts, Seeds and a Couple of Herbs ~ 37

Butternut & Bourbon * Nut of your Choice Praline * Salt & Pepper Cashew Brittle
Toasted Coconut * Marzipan Ice Cream with a choice of Inclusions * Toasted Sesame
Fresh Mint * Lavender

Chocolate ~ 43

How to Melt Chocolate * Dark Chocolate * Chocolate Caramel Semifreddo-ish
Chocolate and Crunchy Peanut Butter Ripple * Dark Chocolate and Candied Orange
Über Mocha * Chocolate-Chilli Ripple * White Chocolate Chip
White Chocolate & Coffee * Chewy Double Chocolate Ripple

Specifically Alcoholic Ice Creams ~ 49

Bramley Apple & Cider * Rum & Raisin * Brandied Cherry & White Chocolate
Prune & Armagnac * Amaretti-Amaretto * Painkiller * 'Ti Punch Ice Cream
Buttered Rum & Ginger * Baileys * Honey Mead Ice Cream
Neat Spirit and Liqueur Ice Creams

Cakes, Biscuits, Meringues and Similar Additions ~ 57

Tutti Frutti * Rocky Road * Elevensies Ice Cream * Chocolate Ginger Crunch
Brown Bread Ice Cream * Hot Cross Bun * Cinnamon Toast * Eton Mess
Peach & Brown Sugar Meringue * Coffee, Kahlua & Squidgy Chocolate Meringue Honey-comb * Fudge Crumble * Chocolate Brownie Caramel Swirl * Stracciatella
Alcoholic by Necessity Trifle Ice Cream * Boodle-ish Orange Fool
Christmas Pudding Ice Cream * Treacle Pudding * Jamaican Gingerbread * Carrot Cake
Banana Rum Cake * Sticky Toffee Pudding

Savoury, Interesting & Peculiar ~ 69

Strawberry Balsamic Ripple * Cracked Black Pepper * Werther's Original Crunch
Popping Candy * Smoky Bacon & Maple Syrup * Blue Cheese
Blue Cheese & Port Ripple * Blue Cheese and Baked Pear * Peppered Blue Cheese
Goats Cheese and Hazelnut * Peppered Goats Cheese Ice Cream
Butternut Squash (or Pumpkin) & Maple Syrup * Roasted Beetroot & Chocolate
Black Garlic Ice Cream

Sauces, Syrups, Coulis & Curds ~ 77

Sticky Chocolate Sauce * Extreme Chocolate Sauce
Dark, Milk or White Chocolate Caramel Sauce * Sticky Toffee Sauce
Apple Cider Sauce * Caramel/Pineapple/Rum Sauce * Lemon, Orange or Lime Curd
Raspberry Curd * Fresh Fruit Sauces, Purees and Coulis * Syrup Recipe + 10 variations
Crystallised Orange * Crystallised Chilli

Inclusions, Complimentary Stuff & Ancillary Recipes ~ 90

How to make Caramel * Roasted/Toasted Nuts * Praline & Brittle * Coffee Brittle
Bacon Brittle * How to Vastly Improve Desiccated Coconut * Crunchy Crumble Topping
Chocolate Bark * Failproof Meringue Recipe * Brown Sugar Meringues
Coffee Meringues * Pink Peppercorn Meringues * Squidgy Chocolate Meringues
Tuiles * Brandy Snaps * Cones

Sexy Ideas & Presentations ~ 100

Sundae Sermon * Affogato* * Coffee Ice Cream melting in a Bittersweet Chocolate Soup
Ice Cream Truffles * Coconut Ice Ice (Baby) * Fruit Shells * Profiteroles * Terrines
Bombes * Baked Alaska * Ice Cream Fritters * Cones, Cornets & Pokes!
Ice Cream Cakes * Ice Cream Tarts * Ice Cream Sandwiches
Milk Shakes * Ice Cream Soda or Float * Ice Cream Cocktails

Summing Up and Endnotes ~ 110

~ *Intro, Info and the Genius Recipe* ~

The following may be a chefs' secret, if so – sorry, everyone!

I do not wish it to be thought that I in any way pooh pooh the ice cream machine; in my time I have found it to be a boon and I do like boons. I once dropped a huge and fabulous strawberry cheesecake, still in its pan, which luckily hit the floor right side up. The filling shot into the air and returned to the base perfectly uncontaminated but in completely the wrong order. Obviously, I couldn't serve it like that so I scraped the whole lot into a handy ice cream machine and shortly afterwards received a delicious and very saleable strawberry cheesecake ice cream. However, …

I have been a chef for ages, over 30 years, the most recent half of them cooking on the lovely little Caribbean island of Tortola. Naturally in all that hot sunshine iced desserts are much in demand and I managed, indeed more than managed to come up with the goods without using an ice cream machine. I haven't been messing with ice and salt ether!

What I have been doing is adapting, tweaking and varying one embarrassingly simple recipe to make numerous delicious and even impressive (at least to me!) ice creams and ice cream dishes. Basic though the method is, many of these ices have been best sellers in high class restaurants and are in no way a compromise.

Having seen how many homemade ice cream books there are on the market, often involving complicated methods and expensive ice cream machines, I felt it would be a shame not to pass on this undemanding but excellent recipe

Incidentally, for the purpose of this book almost all these ice creams have been tested, photographed and even eaten either in a small touring caravan in England or on a small boat in Tortola, such is my nomadic lifestyle and the simplicity of the method.

When I first published this as an eBook I had a few complaints from the other side of the pond as all the recipes were given in metric and all the ingredients had their English names. I have now gone through the whole book adding cup measurements to every-thing. I hope this helps.

Furthermore, here is a list of relevant American alternatives to English ingredients ...

~ Double cream – double cream is 48% butterfat but heavy or heavy whipping cream can be used successfully (and thanks to a reader in France, where the cream is somewhat different I now know that their 30% butterfat 'whipping' cream works too).

~ Condensed milk – sweetened condensed milk.

~ Single cream – light cream

~ Caster sugar – superfine sugar

~ Icing sugar – confectioners or powdered sugar.

~ Desiccated coconut – sadly we don't have sweetened shredded coconut in the UK! No idea why but I have devised a way to improve on our dry and boring desiccated coconut, see page 105. If you are American use sweetened shredded coconut and rejoice!

~ Plain flour – all-purpose flour.

~ Cider – hard cider; in the UK "cider "only refers to the alcoholic drink.

~ Jam – jelly.

- Digestive biscuits – graham crackers.
- Dark chocolate – bittersweet chocolate.
- Cling film – Saran wrap

Two English ingredients that deserve special mention ...

1. Golden Syrup – often corn syrup is recommended as an alternative for this, and it does work, but golden syrup is a by-product of refining sugar cane and has a wonderful caramel-ish flavour. Golden syrup *is* available in the States and well worth searching out.

2. Clotted Cream – luscious, rich (55% butterfat!) and utterly delicious cream made by heating milk then cooling in a shallow pan for several hours during which time the cream rises to the surface and forms a crust. Clotted cream originated in the West Country of England – where I now live – and is not, I believe, available in the States other than in jars which in no way equals the wonderful real thing, so don't bother unless you can get genuine fresh clotted cream.

The Genius Recipe

500ml/2 cups double cream - not the extra thick kind
200g/⅔ cup condensed milk

- Whisk the cream till it is very thick and looks like the picture and then stop. If you go too far it will become butter!
- Fold in the condensed milk.
- Freeze.

If that's all you do you get an ice cream that is not exactly soft scoop but which does have a good texture once it's been out of the freezer a few minutes. It has a pretty blah taste. I can sense your excitement from here but there's even more, I urge you to read on.

Clotted Cream Variation

If you are going to add flavours to this do so abstemiously so that the clotted cream taste shines though, otherwise there's no point in using it.

250ml/1 cup clotted cream
250ml/1 cup single cream
200g/⅔ cup condensed milk

~ Slowly whisk together the two creams till merged and then up the speed and whisk till thick.
~ Fold in the condensed milk.
~ Freeze

This is also a little hard fresh out the freezer but quickly softens and has a rich Cornish cream taste, ideal for serving with strawberries and perhaps a scone.

You will notice that in addition to the two basic ingredients all the following ice creams contain either alcohol or something very sweet, such as a preserve or syrup, or occasionally both. It is sugar, both turned to alcohol and otherwise, that makes for an ice cream that is "soft scoop" straight from the freezer and, of course, the sweet condensed milk goes a long way to help achieve this. If you are making an ice cream based on a sweet addition such as caramel, maple syrup, honey etc. it will be a lovely texture. If your ice cream has alcohol in it, ideally 50ml/3 tablespoons of spirit or liqueur per 500ml/2 cups cream, this too will make for a good creamy consistency.

An ice cream without benefit of either syrup or alcohol will need a little "tempering". This is a technical term meaning to leave your ice cream out of the freezer to soften for a while before you eat it. Whilst it is difficult to give much guidance on tempering times perhaps 30 minutes in the fridge or 10-15 minutes at room temperature, depending on what temperature your room and fridge are, of course. In an emergency I have softened ice cream in the microwave but it is a nerve wracking experience – do it on low for a few seconds at a time. In all cases be prepared to eat the lot if it over-softens as re-freezing can damage the texture.

Oh, and remember that flavours are less pronounced when very cold. It is, therefore, important that your ice cream mixture has a good, strong, bold taste before freezing.

Do please read through each recipe before you make it. They are all variations on a theme but I might say something surprising.

Folding In

It is vital that you do fold rather than stir the condensed milk and any other ingredients into the cream; you want to retain the air that has been whipped in and even to fold in a tad more.

Although it's not easy to explain an action in words, for those of you unsure of how to fold in I'm going to give it a try. Once the cream is thick pour in the condensed milk and anything else that needs folding in, according to the recipe. Using a large metal spoon or a spatula cut across the middle of the cream, slide the spoon or spatula under the cream to the edge of the bowl and fold that portion of the cream over the rest. It's quite simple to do, just hard to describe. Keep cutting and folding from different angles, rotating the bowl, till everything is merged together in a light and airy way. Sometimes if the two components being folded together are of very different consistencies the resulting mixture might be a little lumpy looking. If this happens you can cheat by whisking everything together for no more than six or seven nanoseconds just to even things out.

Marbling

This is achieved by lightly folding together two or more complimentary ice creams of contrasting colours when they are partially frozen to give a marbled effect.

Dulce de Leche

Spanish for sweetness of milk or milk candy or some such thing this is a popular Latin American caramelised milk which is delicious on its own, on toast or in a number of dishes, including in or on ice cream.

There are several ways to bring about dulce de leche in your kitchen and they are:

~ Take whole milk and sugar and simmer or bake it for hours as is traditional.
~ Do the above but instead use condensed milk and no sugar – probably less cooking time too.
~ In a large deep pan cover unopened cans of condensed milk with water. Bring to a boil and simmer, with no lid on, for two or three hours topping up as necessary. Make *absolutely sure* the cans are always covered with water, otherwise they might explode. This tendency has led to dulce de leche being known as "dangerous pudding" in some circles and, therefore, I don't recommend it.
~ Buy the condensed milk already caramelised or dulcéed, so to speak. I heartily recommend this last method. Until this recently came on the market, however, I always used method number 3 with no ill effects whatsoever apart from a bit of a weight problem.

Dulce de leche is a delicious alternative to plain condensed milk in many of these recipes – sometimes I will specify which but the two work equally well, use dulce de leche when you feel its caramel flavour will enhance the finished dish. The method, however, is a wincy bit different as dulce de leche is thicker than plain condensed milk.

500ml/2 cups double cream
200g/⅔ cup dulce de leche/caramelised condensed milk

~ Whisk the cream till it is slightly thickened.
~ Add the dulce de leche and continue whisking, going slowly till the cream and condensed milk have merged. Up the speed and continue till the cream is thick.
~ Continue with the ice cream recipe.

Adding Inclusions

Recipes for all the syrups and sauces needed to make the recipes in this book are in "Sauces, Syrups, Coulis & Curds" on page 77 whilst those for solid inclusions such as meringues, bits of cake etc. are in "Inclusions, Complimentary Stuff & Ancillary Recipes", page 90, although I do sometimes suggest bought in substitutions to make life easier for you. You know what you're like!

To ripple something, say a syrup or a sauce, through an ice cream do so just before freezing, like this … pour the ice cream mixture into your chosen container, drizzle over the sauce or syrup in a figure of 8, or any other enthusiastic swirly shape, and stir it through just once or twice making sure to do a large expansive sort of stir down to the bottom and out to the sides of the mixture. Freeze. When the ice cream is served the cutting, scooping and spooning will cause it to ripple further.

To add crunchy inclusions fold them in together with, or after, the condensed milk. Remember that some inclusions will soften with time so don't plan too far ahead with these ice creams. It is often an attractive idea to keep back a little of the inclusion to sprinkle on top when you serve it.

When adding cake as in the Christmas Pudding Ice Cream lightly fold in the crumbled cake, together with any syrup or sauce in the recipe, after the condensed milk so as not to break up the cake with too much movement.

Freezing and Shelf Life

Basically, you decant your ice cream mixture into a freezer-proof dish and put it in the freezer till frozen. That will work, of course, but here are a few suggestions which might make it work even better.

Freezing the ice cream quickly results in a smoother texture as fewer ice crystals form. It helps, therefore, to have your ingredients very cold before mixing and to chill your bowl and whisk. Shallow containers also speed up freezing.

Use a suitable container; you want something freezer-proof that conducts heat (or in this case cold) well and is, perhaps, attractive to look at if you intend to serve straight from the dish. Obviously square or rectangular containers are better than round for ergonomic storing, although if you are intending to serve a bombe, or other fancy moulded ice cream, then shallow and rectangular go out the window in favour of beautiful.

There's some excellent silicone bakeware on the market these days. Lots of different and interesting shapes and ice cream enhancing colours and, being flexible, it is easy to turn ices out without damaging them.

Make sure there is a little headroom above the surface of the ice cream – it will expand slightly as it freezes.

Press a piece of cling film directly on top of the ice cream, right out to the edges, before putting the lid on. This is to ensure that it does not pick up any other flavours drifting about in the freezer, so that the ice cream doesn't dry out and also to stop ice crystals forming on the surface. If you serve only part of your ice cream re-press the cling film against all its exposed areas before returning to the freezer.

As a general, and not difficult to keep, rule homemade ice cream is better eaten sooner rather than later although it does need a few hours after freezing for the flavours to meld.

Unlike commercial ice cream these recipes contain no stabilisers so don't re-freeze and try to avoid fluctuating temperatures in the freezer as this can cause ice crystals. On the plus side they also contain no egg so are perfect for people with egg allergies.

To my mind the perfect serving temperature for ice cream is 0°F/-18°C although it is probably a good idea to store it a little colder and maybe do a smidge of tempering before serving.

Sphenopalatine Ganglioneuralgia

Of course no book on ice cream would be complete without a mention of this.

Also known as an ice cream headache or brain freeze this is the pain that can strike when eating something very cold.

Apparently it is nothing to do with the brain (except the part that says "must eat ice cream") but is caused by cold food touching the roof of the mouth causing blood vessels in the head to dilate ~ which hurts.

If you can keep the ice cream away from the roof of your mouth you're laughing.

~ *Very, Very Easy Ice Creams* ~

The ice creams in this first chapter are made by simply adding a conserve, preserve, syrup, sauce, honey or other sweet gooey thing to the basic recipe plus, of course, a few variations. The sugary addition will make the ice cream luscious.

Maple Syrup Ice Cream

You thought I'd start with vanilla, didn't you? Maple flavoured syrup, as in Lyle's Maple Flavour Golden Syrup for instance, is even sweeter than pure – use a little less and your ice cream will not be quite so refined, my dear, but still very good indeed.

500ml/2 cups double cream
200g/⅔ cup condensed milk
150ml/⅔ cup maple syrup

~ Whip the cream till thick.
~ Fold in the condensed milk.
~ Fold in the maple syrup.
~ Freeze.

If you happen to be American, and some people are you know, and especially if it is around the fourth Thursday in November serve with Pecan Pie.

Honey Ice Cream

500ml/2 cups double cream
200g/⅔ cup condensed milk
200g/⅔ cup runny honey

~ Whip the cream till thick.
~ Fold in the condensed milk.
~ Fold in the honey.
~ Freeze.

Honey and Ginger Ice Cream

500ml/2 cups double cream
200g/⅔ cup condensed milk
150g/½ cup runny honey
4-5 knobs of stem ginger – finely chopped
50ml/3 tablespoons syrup from the stem ginger jar

~ As above but fold in the chopped ginger and its syrup together with the honey and condensed milk.
~ Freeze.

Honey & Lemon Ice Cream

Try this if you've got a cold, it probably won't work but who cares? Perhaps a tot of whisky poured over might not work either but it's worth a try.

500ml/2 cups double cream
finely grated zest (yellow skin only, no white) and the juice of 2 fine lemons
200g/⅔ cup condensed milk
200g/⅔ cup runny honey

~ Whisk the lemon juice and zest together with the cream till thick.
~ Fold in the condensed milk.
~ Fold in the honey.
~ Freeze.

Lavender Honey Ice Cream

A simple and delicious way to augment the honey is to flavour it with lavender.

200g/⅔ cup runny honey
3 teaspoons of fresh clean lavender flowers, lightly crushed
500ml/2 cups double cream
200g/⅔ cup condensed milk

~ Gently heat together the honey and the lavender for a few minutes. Turn off the heat and leave to infuse for half an hour or so.
~ Strain through a fine sieve – it might be necessary to reheat the honey to get it through the holes. If so, cool to room temperature again. Throw away the lavender.
~ Whip the cream till thick.
~ Fold in the condensed milk.
~ Fold in the honey.
~ Freeze.

For a stronger pure lavender taste see Lavender Ice Cream on page 42.

Greek Yogurt & Honey Ice Cream with optional nuts

This ice cream has a strange quenching quality, like having a long cold drink when thirsty and is difficult to set aside once started. I had considered folding in walnuts or almonds but, for me, they would be an interruption – perhaps better, I think, to sprinkle on after.

280ml/1 cup + 2 tablespoons full fat Greek yogurt
approximately 220ml/a scant cup double cream – enough to make the yogurt up to 500ml/2 cups
200g/⅔ cup condensed milk
200g/⅔ cup runny honey

~ Put the yogurt into a measuring jug and make up to 500ml/2 cups with the cream.
~ Whisk the two together till thick.
~ Fold in the condensed milk.
~ Fold in the honey.
~ Freeze.

Thunder and Lightning Ice Cream

Thunder and Lighting is Cornish for Clotted Cream and Golden Syrup! Just ripple some Golden Syrup through the Clotted Cream Ice Cream recipe on page 4 – there's lovely!

Dulce de Leche Ripple

500ml/2 cups double cream
1 teaspoon pure vanilla extract
200g/⅔ cup dulce de leche/caramel condensed milk PLUS the rest of the can!

~ Whisk together the cream and the vanilla extract till it is slightly thickened.
~ Add 200g dulce de leche and continue whisking till fully incorporated and the mixture is thick.
~ Pour into a container for freezing.
~ Drizzle the rest of the dulce de leche over the ice cream and swirl in a couple of times.
~ Freeze.

Crunchy Peanut Butter Ice Cream

As peanut butter is so very thick and awesome the method is slightly different from usual and, by the way, don't use homemade and/or organic peanut butter; it is too oily, just use some good bought in mass produced stuff. Granulated sugar gives the ice cream added crunch which I like but if you prefer use caster or soft light brown sugar.

400g/1⅔ cup crunchy peanut butter
100g/½ cup sugar
2 teaspoons vanilla extract
200g/⅔ cup dulce de leche/caramelised condensed milk
500ml/2 cups double cream

~ Gently whisk together the peanut butter, sugar, vanilla extract and the dulce de leche to blend.
~ Gradually add the cream whisking slowly till all merged together.
~ Up the speed of your mixer and whisk till the mixture has lightened in colour – this will add air to the ice cream.
~ Freeze.

Peanut Butter & Chocolate Swirl

As above but ripple through up to 200ml/1 cup of your favourite chocolate sauce – Dark Chocolate Caramel Sauce on page 79 is good for this. If you want more chocky and less peanut butter see this recipe for Chocolate and Crunchy Peanut Butter Ripple on page 45.

P. B. & J. I. C.

Peanut Butter and Jelly Ice Cream, of course!

 As above but swirl in up to 200g/⅔ cup of your favourite jam or jelly (American usage) instead of chocolate sauce.

Marmalade

500ml/2 cups double cream
200g/⅔ cup condensed milk
425g/1⅓ cup fine shred marmalade, stirred briefly to liquefy it.

~ Whip the cream till thick.
~ Fold in the condensed milk.
~ Fold in the marmalade.
~ Freeze.

Adding a little Cointreau makes a very soft and delicious ice cream, but one which is less than perfect for breakfast – difficult to keep on the toast.

Jam!

I just wondered what it would be like; jam ice cream. Firstly I tried with some fancy Black Cherry & Port Conserve that had been in the cupboard for … oh some while and it made a surprisingly delicious and sophisticated ice cream. I tried it again with a good quality strawberry jam and it made a surprisingly delicious and sophisticated ice cream. So there you have it. If you also wonder how jam ice cream tastes fold 425g/1⅓ cup of your chosen jam into the cream together with the condensed milk.

Lemon (or indeed orange, lime or raspberry) Curd Ice Cream

Ready-made lemon curd is easily available and even the cheapest makes fairly good ice cream; nice texture but not much lemony tang (which isn't surprising; some of the cheapest I have tried had no lemon in the ingredients!). If using bought in lemon curd I suggest you add the finely grated zest and juice of a lemon to the ice cream. If you want a really bright lemony taste, however, see Lemon Posset Ice Cream on page 22.

Curds of other fruits are not so easy to find. There is a recipe for tangy homemade lemon/lime/orange curd on page 81 plus a slightly different one for raspberries

500ml/2 cups double cream
200g/⅔ cup condensed milk
400g/1¼ cups fruit curd

~ Whip the cream till thick.
~ Fold in the condensed milk.
~ Fold in the fruit curd* and the zest if using.
~ Freeze.

* Maybe keep a little curd back and then ripple it through for added prettiness.

An easy lemon curd variation is Lemon Poppy Seed Ice Cream which has a few tablespoons of poppy seeds folded into the above recipe; just enough to make it pleasantly spotty.

Brandied Mincemeat Ice Cream

500ml/2 cups double cream
200g/⅔ cup condensed milk
350g/1 cup + 1 tablespoon mincemeat
50ml/3 tablespoons brandy

~ Stir the brandy and the mincemeat together vigorously till completely mixed.
~ Whip the cream till thick.
~ Fold in the condensed milk.
~ Fold in the mincemeat and brandy mixture.
~ Freeze.

Toffee Ripple

In the days before home computers, with quick and easy typo corrections and printing, we spent an entire summer with Toffee Nipple Ice Cream on the menu. Surprisingly popular! This recipe is as easy as the others in this chapter but you do have to make the toffee sauce first which takes a matter of minutes, plus cooling. The recipe is on page 79.

500ml/2 cups double cream
200g/⅔ cup condensed milk
1 batch room temperature toffee sauce

~ Whip the cream till thick.
~ Fold in the condensed milk and half of the toffee sauce.
~ Put into an appropriate container.
~ Drizzle over the rest of the toffee sauce and slightly ripple through the ice cream.
~ Freeze.

Nutella Fudge Ripple

After making this ice cream I swirled in the rest of the jar of Nutella and was delighted to find that when the ripples froze they became fudgy. Brilliant!

500ml/2 cups double cream
200g/⅔ cup condensed milk
320g/1 cup Nutella plus another up to 200g/⅔ cup for rippling

~ Whip the cream till thick.
~ Fold in the condensed milk.
~ Fold in the 320g/1 cup Nutella.
~ Decant into a suitable container, dollop over the remaining Nutella and swirl once or twice through the cream.
~ Freeze.

Elderflower Ice Cream

At this point it behoves one to say; "quintessentially English".

500ml/2 cups double cream
240ml/1 cup elderflower cordial
200g/⅔ cup condensed milk

~ Whip together the cream and the elderflower cordial till thick.
~ Fold in the condensed milk.
~ Freeze.

Syrup Ice Creams

Adding flavoured syrup to the basic recipe is another quick and easy way to make delicious ice cream – once you have made the syrup which, however, can be done days or weeks before you need it; the ice cream itself is a doddle. You can, of course, use bought in flavoured syrups although I don't think they are generally speaking as good as homemade; less syrupy and sometimes based on sugar alternatives such as aspartame. There are instructions for lots of different flavour syrups in "Sauces, Syrups, Coulis & Curds"- page 77.

As a guideline and an example, I give the following recipe for Coffee Ice Cream which, I have to say at the risk of being conceited, is utterly delicious.

Coffee Ice Cream

500ml/2 cups double cream
200g/⅔ cup condensed milk
1 teaspoon vanilla extract
120ml/½ cup coffee syrup
a spoonful or two of fresh coffee grounds - optional

~ Whip the cream and the vanilla extract till thick.
~ Fold in the condensed milk.
~ Fold in the coffee syrup and the ground coffee, if using.
~ Freeze.

Good additions to Coffee Ice Cream would be crushed caramel or toasted nuts – see the chapter on Inclusions, page 90 for details.

~ *Slightly More Complicated* ~

And the complication is … adding flavour to the cream before whipping. There is not much work involved but you do need to think ahead.

These recipes require heating the cream together with whatever is providing the flavour, cooling then chilling till really, really cold, e.g. overnight. If the cream is not really cold it will not whip – you have been warned! These infused ice creams are not so successful if made in smaller quantities.

When chilling a flavoured cream lightly press a piece of cling film directly onto its surface so that a skin doesn't form and cause lumps in the finished dish. If infusing a vanilla pod or spices in the cream leave the flavourings in till the cream is cold but then strain out any seeds, pods, sticks, peel etc. *before* chilling or the cream will congeal around them.

The flavoured and cooled cream will be thicker than un-heated cream; for this reason it is easiest to whisk the condensed milk in as the cream thickens rather than fold in after.

~ Slightly More Complicated ~

Double Vanilla Ice Cream

For many years my sister Maggie and I, in conjunction with our then-husbands, were partners in a beachside hotel in Cornwall which had a seaside shop. In this shop we sold 20 flavours of ice cream which was pretty good in the 1980s.

Although they were all popular, we generally found that ladies favoured Maple Walnut whilst gentlemen preferred the manly taste of Rum and Raisin. Children wanted Mint-Choc-Chip and teenagers, if you could get them to say anything, mumbled "umm – Strawberry". Senior citizens usually wanted "plain", by which they meant vanilla, and told us their preference in tones of irritated amazement as if it was obvious that ice cream should be "plain vanilla". What was the world coming to?

The thing is; vanilla isn't plain at all, is it? A vanilla pod is the seed pod from the vanilla orchid, mainly *vanilla planifolia* from Central America, Mexico and Madagascar but occasionally other strains from Tahiti and Hawaii. It is, therefore, very exotic and sexy and is also delicious. Please don't diss the vanilla orchid. Always use real *pure* vanilla extract in any recipes that ask for vanilla essence. It is more expensive but a little goes a long way and I'm sure you won't regret it. Even better is a vanilla pod and the best vanilla pod is a nice soft, shiny, bendy one.

I have called this Double Vanilla as my original vanilla ice cream, which was purely vanilla infused cream and condensed milk, was a little on the firm side. I tried folding in some vanilla syrup and that was much more luxurious.

500ml/2 cups double cream
1 vanilla pod
200g/⅔ cup condensed milk
80ml/⅓ cup vanilla syrup – see page 85

~ Cut the vanilla pod in half lengthways and put into a small pan together with the cream.
~ Bring to just under boiling point, turn off the heat, cover and leave to infuse the flavour of the vanilla as the cream cools.
~ Remove the vanilla pod and scrape the tiny black seeds from it into the cold cream. Keep the vanilla pod – see below.
~ Chill the cream to very cold.
~ Whisk the vanilla cream to thick and fold in the condensed milk and the vanilla syrup.
~ Freeze.

The vanilla pod can be rinsed, dried and stored in a container of sugar to make vanilla sugar, if you are that sort of a person, or in a bottle of rum or brandy if you are *that* sort of person.

Even simpler but not quite as good and not so pretty is just to whisk a teaspoon of pure vanilla extract in with the cream before folding in the condensed milk and syrup.

Island Spice Ice Cream

I get lovely fresh spices, some even home-grown, in the Caribbean but excellent alternatives are easy to find at home too. Serve with something tropical such as grilled pineapple, bananas cooked in rum and brown sugar or an exotic fruit salad.

2 cinnamon sticks
12 whole cloves
1 orange
200g/⅔ cup condensed milk
1 teaspoon pure vanilla extract
3 tablespoons rum - obviously a spiced rum is particularly good

~ With a potato peeler carefully remove the zest from the orange in long strips. Try not to get any of the white pith that is under the zest as this can be bitter.
~ Put the zest into a small pan together with the cloves, cinnamon sticks and cream.
~ Bring to *just* under boiling point. Turn off the heat, cover and leave to infuse the flavours till lukewarm.
~ Strain the cream, discarding the spices and zest.
~ Chill the cream till completely and utterly cold.
~ Whisk the cream together with the rum and vanilla extract till thick.
~ Fold in the condensed milk as usual.
~ Freeze.

~ Slightly More Complicated ~

Liquorice Ice Cream

Star anise is a predominant flavour in liquorice and Pernod is that way inclined too.

500ml/2 cups double cream
4 whole star anise
1 strip lemon zest
a drip or two of black food dye - optional
200g/⅔ cup condensed milk
3 tablespoons Pernod
100g/3½ oz of soft liquorice – coarsely chopped

~ Put the cream into a small pan together with the star anise and lemon zest.
~ Bring to just under boiling point. Turn off the heat and leave to infuse the flavours till lukewarm.
~ Strain the cream, setting aside the star anise and discarding the zest.
~ Chill the cream to completely and utterly cold.
~ Whisk the cream together with the Pernod, and food colouring if using, till thick.
~ Fold in the condensed milk and the liquorice.
~ Freeze.

Rinse and dry the star anise and use as a pretty garnish for the ice cream or some other dish.

Salty Liquorice Ice Cream

I am reliably informed by a Canadian friend that salted liquorice is considered a delicacy in Canada so try adding a pinch of crunchy sea salt to the Liquorice Ice Cream. This is just a suggestion – I haven't tried it!

Lemon Posset Ice Cream

Lemon Posset is a very simple old English recipe which makes a deliciously fresh and tangy ice cream, less rich than the one made with lemon curd in the previous chapter. In fact even simper is not to even bother making the ice cream! Just stop when you have made the posset which is a lovely dessert as it is but, you know, ice cream book and all that.

500ml/2 cups double cream
110g/½ cup sugar
finely grated zest and the juice of 4 lovely lemons
200g/⅔ cup condensed milk

~ Mix together the cream and the sugar in a small pan and bring to just under the boil, stirring till the sugar has dissolved.
~ Remove from the heat and whisk in the lemon zest and juice which will cause the cream to thicken.
~ Set aside to cool and then chill till completely cold (eat now or continue to the next stage!).
~ Whisk till thick and fold in the condensed milk.
~ Freeze.

See Boodle-ish Orange Fool Ice Cream on page 65 for a similar recipe using oranges.

Lemon Meringue Ice Cream

Turn the above recipe into Lemon Meringue Ice Cream by folding in crumbled meringues before freezing. This also works with the Lemon Curd Ice Cream on page 15 but using this recipe is even better; the creamy sharpness contrasted by the sugary crunch is divine. See page 94 for meringue recipes and information.

~ Slightly More Complicated ~

St. Clément's Ice Cream

Another pleasant contrast is to ripple Lemon Posset Ice Cream through with orange syrup and add crystallised orange pieces (page 88) before freezing.

Cocoa Nib (Crunch) Ice Cream

This has an intriguing flavour which is reminiscent of rather than *actually* of chocolate; it is delicate, subtle and delicious, best relished with no distractions. However, if you then sugar crust some more cocoa nibs, crush them and add to the ice cream it assumes a dark chocolatey taste and crunch.

Please note that this recipe takes 600ml of cream because the cocoa nibs seem to absorb some which needs to be replaced.

600ml/2½ cups double cream
200g/⅔ cup cocoa nibs – divided into two x 100g/⅓ cup
200g/⅔ cup condensed milk
½ teaspoon vanilla syrup
85g/½ cup light brown sugar

~ Put 100g/⅓ cup cocoa nibs into a small non-stick pan together with the cream.
~ Bring to just under boiling point, turn off the heat and leave to infuse as it cools.
~ Strain and discard the cocoa nibs.
~ Press a piece of cling film onto the surface of the cream and chill till utterly cold.

Whilst it is cooling …

~ Set a lightly greased baking tray beside the stove.
~ Put the other 100g/⅓ cup cocoa nibs into a small pan together with the sugar.
~ Stir together over medium heat until most of the sugar has melted and it is clinging to the nibs.
~ Turn out onto the baking tray, spread out in a single layer and leave to cool and set.
~ Crush lightly (or heavily if you prefer).

To assemble …

~ Whip the flavoured cream.
~ Fold in the condensed milk and the vanilla syrup.

- Fold in the sugared cocoa nibs, if using, maybe saving back a few for garnish.
- Freeze.

Caramel Ice Cream

Caramel takes quite a while to reach the correct colour and does need almost constant attention so may I suggest a few gentle stretching exercises whilst you stare at it?

> 100g/½ cup white sugar
> 60ml/¼ cup water
> 500ml/2 cups double cream
> 200g/⅔ cup condensed milk

- Set the cream beside the stove.
- In a deep saucepan over low heat stir together the sugar and the water till the sugar is dissolved and then bring to a boil. Don't stir any more but when it begins turning golden you can swirl it about a bit to even out the colour.
- Cook to a deep golden brown watching carefully and swirling occasionally.
- As soon as it reaches this colour, all at once yet carefully (it will boil rapidly) add the cream and stir over low heat till the caramel, which will have hardened and gone all interesting, has melted back into the cream. Don't re-boil the cream as this will reduce it and make less ice cream!
- Cool then chill thoroughly – overnight would be a good idea.
- When the cream is utterly cold whisk till thick and fold in the condensed milk.
- Freeze.

Caramelised Cinnamon Ice Cream

Well, hardly a recipe – just whisk in some ground cinnamon, to taste, with the cream. I suggest about a half a teaspoon per batch but if you like a stronger taste add a bit more. This is very apple pie friendly.

~ Slightly More Complicated ~

Salted Caramel Crunch Ice Cream

Salted caramel is quite fashionable now but will probably still be delicious when the fad has passed. Make caramel in accordance with the instructions on page 91 and as soon as you have poured the caramel out to cool sprinkle with a generous pinch of crunchy sea salt. When cold crush, fold into the Caramel Ice Cream above and freeze. Of course, you could leave out the salt and just have Caramel Crunch Ice Cream.

Brown Sugar Ice Cream

I have made this with soft light brown sugar and with soft dark brown sugar and there is little difference in the result except one is a lighter brown than the other. Both are delicious; dark brown sugar has *maybe* a little more flavour but perhaps I imagined it.

60g/½ stick butter
120g/⅔ cup soft brown sugar
pinch of salt
500ml/2 cups double cream
½ teaspoon vanilla extract
200g/⅔ cup condensed milk

~ Heat together the butter, sugar and salt stirring, till the butter has melted – and so has the sugar.
~ Add the vanilla extract and the cream and stir till all merged into one light brown colour. Do not boil.
~ Cool then chill till really, really cold.
~ Whip the cream and then fold in the condensed milk.
~ Freeze.

~ *Fruits* ~

If you do nothing but add fresh fruit to the basic recipe you will get a very firm ice cream with crunchy fruit in it – quite refreshing but hardly luscious. As you know for lushness you need something sugary. This being the case I suggest here several ways to more deliciously incorporate fruit into the ice cream.

With soft summer fruits the following simple method produces a lovely pure flavour and a slightly crunchy effect which becomes less apparent as the ice cream relaxes. Either fold all the sauce into the ice cream or keep a little back for rippling then, as the ice cream softens slightly, the ripples become bright pockets of juice amongst the creaminess.

Simple Strawberry Ice Cream

500g/4cups sliced fresh strawberries
250g/1¼ cups sugar
juice of ½ an orange
500ml/2 cups double cream
200g/⅔ cup condensed milk

~ Mash or purée strawberries. Add the sugar and orange juice and stir until the sugar has dissolved.
~ Chill for at least an hour but several hours or overnight is fine.
~ Whip the cream till thick and fold in the condensed milk.
~ Fold in the fruit sauce.
~ Freeze.

Raspberry Ripple

500g/4 cups fresh raspberries
250g/1¼ sugar
juice of 1 lemon
500ml/2 cups double cream
200g/⅔ cup condensed milk

~ Mash or purée the raspberries. Add the sugar and lemon juice and stir until the sugar has dissolved.
~ Chill for at least an hour.
~ Pass the fruit and its juices through a nylon sieve, pressing on the fruit to get as much through the sieve as possible.
~ Whip the cream till thick and fold in the condensed milk.
~ Fold in the half of the fruit sauce.
~ Pour into a container.
~ Ripple in the other half of the sauce.
~ Freeze.

Iced Blueberry Fool

Pretty much the same recipe as above but I've changed the name to keep it interesting!

500g/2½ cups fresh blueberries
250g/1¼ cups sugar
500ml/2 cups double cream
1 tsp vanilla extract
200g/⅔ cup condensed milk

- Mash or purée the blueberries.
- Add the sugar and stir until it has dissolved.
- Chill for at least an hour but overnight is fine too.
- Strain or not, according to your whim.
- Whip the cream and the vanilla extract till thick and fold in the condensed milk.
- Fold in the fruit sauce – it is quite runny, by the way, but folds in fine.
- Freeze.

Peaches & Cream Ice Cream

I once made, or at least tried to make, a celebratory dessert for a summer wedding. I poached fresh peaches in pink champagne intending to make a sorbet with some of the poaching liquid and to serve the peaches and their sorbet in pink heart shaped meringues drizzled with the rest of the pink Champagne syrup. I'm dead posh, me. Sadly, one of the waiters (you know who you are) drank the juices as they were cooling before I could make the sorbet.

Peaches are easily peeled if you drop them into boiling water for 30 seconds and then use a slotted spoon to transfer them to a bowl of iced water. Leave for a minute, drain and dry and their skins will come off no trouble.

8 ripe peaches – peeled, stoned and chopped
150g/¾ cup sugar
80ml/⅓ cup peach schnapps – optional but yum
500ml/2 cups double cream
200g/⅔ cup condensed milk

- Purée the peaches together with the sugar and schnapps (if using).
- Set aside in the fridge for an hour or so.
- Whip the cream till thick and fold in the condensed milk.

~ Fold in all the fruit sauce or keep a little back and ripple in just before freezing.
~ Freeze.

Peach Melba Ripple

Named, as you probably know, after Dame Nellie Melba who must have been quite a girly because Melba Toast was also named after her. To make her eponymous ice cream simply ripple raspberry coulis (see page 82) through Peaches and Cream Ice Cream.

Papaya & Ginger Ice Cream

I only made this because I found a perfectly ripe papaya in the supermarket for 10p! This ice cream is not only a good flavour but also a pretty colour.

500g/3 cups diced fresh papaya flesh
250g/1¼ cups sugar
juice of 1 lime
500ml/2 cups double cream
200g/⅔ cup condensed milk
80ml/⅓ cup ginger syrup – page 86

~ Purée the papaya flesh together with the sugar, the ginger syrup and the lime juice.
~ Set aside in the fridge for an hour or so.
~ Whip the cream till thick and fold in the condensed milk.
~ Fold in all the fruit sauce or keep a little back and ripple in just before freezing.
~ Freeze.

Slightly less delicate fruits benefit from cooking in the sugar syrup to break them down a bit. This is a good way to use up leftover stewed fruit; about 400g/3 cups per full recipe batch or check out these recipes.

Wild Blackberry Ice Cream

As I write this our Cornish lanes are rife with blackberries and this ice cream makes a pleasant change from blackberry and apple crumble, good though that is.

450g/3½ cups blackberries
200g/1 cup sugar
120ml/½ cup water
500ml/2 cups double cream
200g/⅔ cup condensed milk

~ Put the blackberries, sugar and water into a small pan and cook together over medium heat, stirring, until the berries have broken down and gone all squashy.
~ Mash the berries into their juices.
~ If you want to remove the seeds strain through a nylon sieve pressing on the fruit till you have extracted as much loveliness as possible.
~ Cool and chill.
~ Beat the double cream till thick.
~ Fold in the condensed milk.
~ Fold in the blackberry purée, either completely or to achieve a rippled effect.
~ Freeze.

Rhubarb Ice Cream

Incidentally rhubarb is not a fruit, it is a vegetable; a delicious fruity vegetable.

500ml/2 cups double cream
200g/⅔ cup condensed milk
775g/5 cups young rhubarb (the pinker the rhubarb the prettier the ice cream) trimmed and with the tough outer skin and fibres stripped off - sliced
340g/1⅔ cups sugar

~ Put the rhubarb into a saucepan together with the sugar. Add a tablespoon of water just to get it started.
~ Bring to a boil, turn down the heat, cover and simmer, stirring frequently, till all the rhubarb has melted into a pink and stringy syrup! Yum.
~ Cool.
~ Whisk the cream till thick

~ Fold in the condensed milk, fruit and juices.
~ Freeze.

Sautéed Peach and Brown Sugar Ice Cream

I use the lovely little sweet white flat peaches, called Doughnut Peaches, for this but an equivalent weight of "normal" peaches would be a fine alternative.

8 or 10 not too ripe doughnut peaches – coarsely chopped (no need to peel first)
60g/½ stick butter
100g/½ cup soft light brown sugar
a drip or two of vanilla extract
500ml/2 cups double cream
200g/⅔ cup condensed milk

~ Sauté the chopped peach in the butter till very tender and maybe starting to take a little colour
~ Add the sugar and vanilla and stir all together till the sugar has melted.
~ Set aside to cool completely.
~ When cold whisk the cream till stiff.
~ Fold in the condensed milk and the cooked peaches plus every single drop of their juices.
~ Freeze.

Toffee Apple Ice Cream

500g/3 cups peeled cored and diced apples
110g/½ cup sugar
60ml/¼ cup water
75ml/⅓ cup water, apple juice or cider
500ml/2 cups double cream
200g/⅔ cup condensed milk - dulce de leche variety
1 batch of crushed caramel – see page 91 – optional

~ Set the apple juice beside the stove.
~ In a saucepan over low heat stir together the sugar and the water till the sugar is dissolved then bring to a boil. Don't stir any more but when it begins turning colour you can swirl it about a bit to even out the colour.
~ Boil to a deep golden brown watching carefully, swirling occasionally.

~ As soon as it reaches this colour, all at once yet carefully (it will boil rapidly) add the extra water, apple juice or cider and stir over medium heat till the caramel melts back into the sauce.
~ Bring back to a boil, add the chopped diced apple and simmer for about 15 minutes till the apple is tender and there is a little juice remaining.
~ Cool.
~ Make the basic dulce de leche based ice cream, page 6, and fold in the cooked apple and any juices.
~ Fold in the crushed caramel if using.

Burnt Orange Ice

Not really burnt, of course, unless you don't concentrate.

3 oranges
110g/½ cup sugar
60ml/¼ cup water
500ml/2 cups double cream
200g/⅔ cup condensed milk - dulce de leche variety

~ Finely grate the zest of the oranges, just the orange part – no bitter white pith – on the finest grater holes you can find and set aside.
~ Top and tail the oranges and, using a small knife, cut the pith from the orange in strips from top to bottom, thus disclosing the fruit segments.
~ Using the same small knife cut between the membranes and the flesh separating the segments and remove them. Chop coarsely.
~ Squeeze all orange debris into a measuring jug to extract as much juice as possible.
~ Make the juice up to 150ml/⅔ cup with further fresh orange juice or water and set beside the stove.
~ In a saucepan over low heat stir together the sugar and the water till the sugar is dissolved and bring to a boil. Don't stir any more but when it begins turning colour you can swirl it about a bit.
~ Simmer to a deep golden brown watching carefully, swirling occasionally.
~ As soon as it reaches this colour, all at once yet carefully (it will boil rapidly) add the orange juice and stir over medium heat till the caramel melts back into the orange juice.
~ Bring back to a boil, add the chopped orange pieces and simmer for about 10 minutes till the sauce has reduced to a syrup.
~ Cool, add the orange zest and then chill.
~ Make the basic dulce de leche based ice cream (page 6) and fold in the orange

pieces and syrup.
~ Freeze

Port & Orange Ice Cream

~ Ripple through a modicum of Port Syrup (page 88) before freezing.
~ Freeze.

Roasting fruit intensifies its flavour whilst still producing a luscious syrup to mix into the ice cream.

Rum Roasted Banana Ice Cream

45g/3 tablespoons butter
4 ripe bananas
240g/1½ cups light brown sugar
500ml/2 cups double cream
3 tablespoons + an extra 2 tablespoons of rum
200g/⅔ cup condensed milk

~ Preheat oven to 180°C/350°F/160°C fan/gas 4.
~ Peel and thinly slice the bananas.
~ Melt the butter in a shallow oven proof dish (easiest done but putting the butter in the pan in the oven for a few minutes).
~ Add the sliced bananas and the sugar to the melted butter and toss all together.
~ Roast till soft and caramelised and, it has to be said, a bit mushy – about 25 minutes. Stir once or twice during cooking.
~ Add 2 tablespoons of rum and return to oven for 5 minutes.
~ Cool then mash or purée the bananas and their juices.
~ Whisk together the cream and the 3 tablespoons of rum.
~ Fold in the condensed milk and the banana purée.
~ Freeze.

Banana Fudge Ice Cream

Ripple some Nutella or a chocolate sauce of your choice (Sticky Chocolate Sauce on page 78 would be good for this) through the Rum Roasted Banana recipe just before freezing.

Honey Roasted Fig Ice Cream

a little butter
7 fresh figs – quartered
2 tablespoons of light brown sugar
1 tablespoon of runny honey
a drip or two of vanilla extract
500ml/2 cups double cream
200g/⅔ cup condensed milk of your choice

~ Preheat the oven to 200°C/400°F/180°C fan/gas 6.
~ Lightly butter an ovenproof dish.
~ Toss together the figs, sugar, honey and vanilla and bake for about 20 minutes till starting to caramelise.
~ Mash or purée the figs and their juices and set aside to cool.
~ Whisk the cream till thick.
~ Fold in the condensed milk, the figs and their juices.
~ Freeze.

Butterscotch Baked Pear Ice Cream

8 ripe, but still a little firm, pears
170g/1½ sticks butter
170g/1 cup soft light brown sugar
pinch salt
1 teaspoon vanilla extract
500ml/2 cups double cream
200g/⅔ cup condensed milk – preferably dulce de leche version

~ Preheat oven to 180°C/350°F/160°C fan/gas 4
~ Peel and core the pears and cut into 1cm/½"-ish chunks.
~ Put the butter, sugar and salt into a shallow oven proof dish and warm in the oven for a few minutes till melted.
~ Toss the pear pieces in the buttery goo to coat.
~ Cover with foil and bake for about 45-60 minutes till the pears are tender and reclining in a butterscotch sauce.
~ Stir in the vanilla extract.
~ Cool a little and then purée – chunky or smooth, up to you.
~ Whisk the cream and the caramelised condensed milk till thick.

~ Fold in the pear purée.
~ Freeze.

Mango-Lime Ice Cream

The fruit flavour in this is so fresh and sparkling that the ice cream tastes almost fizzy!

2 large ripe mangoes – peeled and coarsely chopped
2 washed and dried limes
100g/½ cup sugar
500ml/2 cups double cream
200g/⅔ cup condensed milk

~ Finely grate the zest (just the green skin, none of the white pith underneath) of the limes and set aside.
~ Squeeze the juice into a small pan and stir in the sugar.
~ Bring to a boil stirring till the sugar has dissolved then simmer together for 3 or 4 minutes.
~ Add the reserved zest to the simmering lime juice and cook another minute or so.
~ Add the chopped mango, return to a simmer and cook until you have a bit of a syrupy situation going on – about 3 minutes
~ Mash or purée as you prefer – for a chunky or smooth ice.
~ Cool completely.
~ Whisk the cream till thick.
~ Fold in the condensed milk and then the mango sauce.
~ Freeze.

Slow Roasted Pineapple with Vanilla (or chilli or cinnamon or nothing) Ice Cream

To prepare a pineapple cut off the top 1cm/½" or so including the crown of leaves. If you are planning to do something fabulous with your pineapple dish you might like to save this in the fridge to use as a centrepiece or garnish. Cut off the base too. Stand the fruit on one end and using a good sharp knife cut downwards in strips to remove the outer skin.

Now remove any little brown "eyes" in the fruit by either removing individually with the point of a small sharp knife, or, if they run in straight lines, which they often do, cut out a thin strip containing several eyes at a time. Halve or quarter the pineapple and remove the core.

Some people like to suck or chew on this whilst thinking about their next move but do be careful – it is said in the West Indies that this can make you pregnant, or at least help to, especially if you are a girl.

> 1 pineapple peeled, prepared and sliced
> 120g/⅔ cup light brown sugar
> 120ml/½ cup water
> 1 vanilla pod (or 1 dried chilli or a cinnamon stick or nothing)
> 500ml/2 cups double cream
> 200g/⅔ cup condensed milk of your choice

~ Preheat the oven to 180°C/350°F/160°C fan/gas 4.
~ Put the sugar and the water into a small pan and stir over low heat till the sugar has dissolved.
~ Up the heat, bring to a boil and then simmer till the liquid has reduced slightly to a light syrup – about 5 minutes.
~ Lay the pineapple slices, overlapping in a shallow ovenproof pan and pour over the syrup.
~ Add your vanilla pod, dried chilli, cinnamon stick or nothing.
~ Bake for about an hour, turning the pineapple occasionally and checking the syrup hasn't reduced too much. Add a little hot water if it has as you need some syrup to stir into the ice cream later. It is ready when sticky and tender and maybe a little golden round the edges.
~ Cool.
~ Remove the vanilla pod (rinse and dry and use for something else) or whatever and coarsely chop the pineapple reserving every single drop of syrup.
~ Whisk the cream till thick.
~ Fold in the condensed milk, the pineapple and all the syrup.
~ Freeze.

There is yet another way to make a luscious fruit ice cream but for that you must read the chapter concerning alcohol on page 49.

~ *Nuts, Seeds and a Couple of Herbs* ~

You will see that several of these recipes contain alcohol. This is because nuts are not by nature juicy and alcohol not only enhances their flavour it also improves the ice cream's texture.

Butternut & Bourbon (as in Buttered Nuts, not the squash) Ice Cream

200g/2 cups coarsely, but not too coarsely, chopped pecans
¼ tsp salt
170g/1½ sticks unsalted butter
500ml/2 cups double cream
1 tsp pure vanilla extract
3 tablespoons Bourbon
200g/⅔ cup condensed milk

~ Preheat the oven to 180ºC/350ºF/160ºC fan/gas 4.
~ Spread the pecans in one layer on a baking tray and put in the oven till they are fragrant and a little darker. This takes about 10 minutes but do watch carefully, too dark and they will be bitter.
~ Add the salt and the butter and toss all tog till the butter has melted and the nuts are coated. Set aside to cool completely.
~ Whip the cream together with vanilla extract and the Bourbon.
~ Fold in the nuts and condensed milk.
~ Freeze.

Nut of Your Choice Praline Ice Cream

Praline is ground up caramel crusted nuts; see here page 92 for the recipe.

When making this ice cream try to match the texture-enhancing alcohol to the chosen nut e.g. Frangelica with hazelnuts, Amaretto with almonds, Bourbon seems right for pecans and brandy for most things.

500ml/2 cups double cream
3 tablespoons suitable liqueur or spirit
200g/⅔ cup condensed milk
225g/2 cups praline – crushed

~ Whisk together the cream and chosen liqueur till thick.
~ Fold in the condensed milk and praline.
~ Freeze.

Salt and Pepper Cashew Brittle Ice Cream

Similar to above but use coarsely chopped salted cashews in the praline and replace the liqueur with 80ml/⅓ cup of Black Pepper Syrup – see page 85.

Toasted Coconut Ice Cream

Apparently, a coconut is a seed rather than a nut despite its name and being bloody enormous.

This ice cream was a staple on my menus in the Caribbean, using sweetened shredded coconut and always served with Caramel/Pineapple/Rum Sauce (page 80). The same recipe in the UK using desiccated coconut has been such a disappointment – too hard, too dry and too tasteless. Luckily, I came up with a way of really improving desiccated coconut – see page 93 – and the resulting ice cream is better than ever.

500ml/2 cups double cream
3 tablespoons rum or coconut rum such as Malibu
200g/⅔ cup condensed milk
320g/4 cups sweetened flaked coconut OR 1 batch of Vastly Improved Desiccated Coconut – page 93

~ Preheat oven to 180ºC/350ºF/160ºC fan/gas 4.
~ Spread the coconut in a shallow pan or tray and bake for about 10 minutes, checking and stirring often, till a lot of it is golden brown. The sugar in the coconut will make it burn easily so be astute.
~ Cool.
~ Whisk together the cream and the rum till thick.
~ Fold in the condensed milk together with almost all the toasted coconut – keep a little back to sprinkle on when serving.
~ Freeze.

Toasted Sesame Ice Cream

100g/⅔ cup sesame seeds
85g/½ cup light brown sugar
500ml/2 cups double cream
200g/⅔ cup condensed milk

~ Cook the sesame seeds in a dry frying pan over medium heat till lightly toasted and smelling good – just a few minutes.
~ Add the sugar and stir about over the heat till the sugar is melted and caramelised and the seeds are starting to clump together.
~ Set aside about half of the seeds and add 250ml/1 cup of cream to those left in the pan.
~ Set aside to cool.
~ Stir the rest of the cream into the cooled mixture, strain and chill.
~ Whip the cream till thick, fold in the condensed milk and the reserved sugary seeds.
~ Freeze.

Marzipan Ice Cream with a choice of Inclusions

200g/7 oz white marzipan
500ml/2 cups double cream
3 tablespoons Amaretto or brandy
200g/⅔ cup condensed milk
up to 400g/14 oz of inclusions – see below

~ Coarsely grate the marzipan and then heat gently with the cream till melted. Cool to completely cold.
~ Whisk together the marzipanned cream and the liqueur to thick.
~ Fold in the condensed milk plus any inclusions.
~ Freeze.

I have tried this with toasted almond praline (page 92) folded in and with brandied cherries – see Brandied Cherry & White Chocolate Ice Cream on page 50 – and with both! It's all good.

A Couple of Herb Ice Creams

I have been surprised recently to discover there is a strain of cannabis plant known as Ice Cream and I would like to stress, at the risk of disappointment, that this book does not include any recipes for their crop. Sorry about that.

Fresh Mint Ice Cream

One of the first ice creams I made using the basic recipe was Fresh Mint Ice Cream and to be frank I didn't like it much. It was so very popular, however, both in the restaurant and in the kitchen with people clamouring to scrape the bowl (sometimes before I'd emptied it) that I had trouble keeping up with demand. The reason I'm not keen is that it is made with fresh mint from the garden which gives a kind of spearmint flavour that is not for me unless accompanied by lamb – hmm, now there's a thought.

200g/2 cups sugar
300ml/1¼ cups water
2 handfuls of fresh mint – men's hands might be best if you have some!
juice of 2 lemons
500ml/2 cups double cream
200g/⅔ cup condensed milk

~ Bring the water and sugar to a boil and boil for 3 minutes to form a syrup.
~ Cool.
~ Wash and drain the mint and put into a liquidizer goblet - pour in the syrup.
~ Puree completely and then strain well through a nylon sieve.
~ Add the lemon juice.
~ Whisk the cream till thick.
~ Fold in the condensed milk and the mint syrup.
~ Freeze.

Hey y'all, if you whisk 3 tablespoons Bourbon in with the cream you have a kind of Mint Julep Ice Cream.

Lavender Ice Cream

The easiest way to get the lavender flavour into the ice cream is to use lavender syrup (page 86). Not surprisingly this has quite a strong lavender taste, if you want something milder see Lavender Honey Ice Cream on page 11.

~ *Chocolate* ~

Although I say in these recipes to melt the chocolate, cocoa and condensed milk together "until smooth" I don't necessarily mean it! I used to make Chocolate Mousse marbled with Cream and Brandy which was always been quite a good seller. For some reason the chocolate never melts smoothly in that particular recipe. After a while, in the interests of honesty, I started calling it "Chocolate Mousse marbled with Cream and Brandy – with inexplicable but delicious little lumps of chocolate in it". It then became *A Really Good Seller*. It is rare to meet a person who isn't delighted to find a lump of chocolate um … well, anywhere really. So, if the mixture doesn't melt completely smoothly and you have lumps of chocolate in your ice cream – rejoice!

Having said that here is some important information on …

How to Melt Chocolate

~ Break the chocolate into a small heatproof bowl and put the bowl into a small pan of simmering water so that the water comes about a third of the way up the sides, and here's a handy hint' – if your bowl is plastic it is a good idea to stand it on a metal jam jar lid or similar to stop it sticking to the bottom of the pan.
~ White chocolate is a little more delicate than dark and must be melted carefully over very low heat.
~ Don't mess with the chocolate as it melts, just let it sit there till it's ready.
~ If you get water into the melting chocolate it will "seize" and go all hard and lumpy and useless and you will have to start again with fresh chocolate. God knows what you will do with the seized stuff.
~ Similarly you don't want to put a lid on the pan whilst the chocolate is melting as steam, which will form, is also water and is particularly watery when it condenses on the lid and falls into the chocolate.

Dark Chocolate Ice Cream

The optional brandy in this recipe benefits the ice cream in two ways; it will make it softer and also taste more ~~alcoholic~~ chocolatey.

The method of whisking the cream is slightly different in this recipe; similar to the dulce de leche method.

200g/⅔ cup condensed milk
175g/1½ cups coarsely chopped dark chocolate
1 tablespoon cocoa
500ml/2 cups double cream
3 tablespoons brandy – optional but highly recommended

~ Put the condensed milk, the chocolate and the cocoa into a small bowl.
~ Stand the bowl in a small pan of water as described above.
~ Simmer the water till the chocolate has melted and then stir smoothly into the condensed milk. This will be quite a thick mixture.
~ Cool slightly but not too much as it needs to be soft enough to fold into the cream.
~ Whip together the cream and the optional brandy till slightly thick.
~ Add the melted chocolate mixture and continue whisking till thick.
~ Freeze

~ Chocolate ~

Chocolate Caramel Semifreddo-ish Ice

This makes a softer, richer chocolate ice cream that doesn't freeze very firmly and is velvety, chocolatey and luxurious. It is not a traditional semifreddo which is made by folding whipped cream into ice cream, but it is certainly half frozen – a sort of wonderful icy mousse.

150g/¾ cup white sugar
80ml/⅓ cup water
200g/1⅔ cups coarsely chopped dark chocolate
1 tsp vanilla extract
500ml/2 cups double cream
200g/⅔ cup condensed milk

~ Set the cream beside the stove.
~ In a deep saucepan over low heat stir together the sugar and the water till the sugar is dissolved and then bring to a boil. Don't stir any more but when it begins turning golden you can swirl it about a bit to even out the colour.
~ Cook to a deep golden brown watching carefully and swirling occasionally.
~ As soon as it reaches this colour, all at once yet carefully (it will boil rapidly) add the cream and stir over low heat till the caramel, which will have hardened has melted back into the cream.
~ When the caramel has melted back into the cream add the chocolate and stir till this too has melted.
~ Stir in the vanilla extract.
~ Cool and chill thoroughly till very cold.
~ Whisk the chocolate cream till thick.
~ Fold in the condensed milk.
~ Freeze.

Chocolate and Crunchy Peanut Butter Ripple

For less chocolate and more peanuts see Peanut Butter and Chocolate Swirl on page 13.

1 x Dark Chocolate Ice Cream – above
5 tablespoons of crunchy-as-you like commercially made peanut butter
2 tsp vanilla extract
1 tablespoon soft dark brown sugar

~ Make the chocolate ice cream.
~ Gently warm together the peanut butter, the sugar and the vanilla essence in a small pan over low heat till it is runny.
~ Put the ice cream into your chosen container.
~ Drizzle the runny peanut butter on top of the ice cream and swirl in a bit to ripple through the ice cream.
~ Freeze.

Dark Chocolate and Candied Orange

This is a bit Jaffa. Use as much candied orange as you like, within reason, because it is lovely biting into the sharp, crunchy, sugary pieces in the midst of all that creamy chocolate. I did try making this with Cointreau as well and it tasted fine but was a little too soft. The recipe for orange syrup and orange peel are on page 88.

1 x Dark Chocolate Ice Cream recipe (above) but without the brandy
5 tablespoons orange syrup
at least one batch of crystallised orange zest – coarsely chopped

~ Make chocolate ice cream.
~ Fold the orange syrup and the candied orange into the whipped cream together with the melted chocolate mixture.
~ Freeze.

Über Mocha

If you have been reading this book with even a modicum of attention you will be expecting me to suggest a coffee liqueur such as Tia Maria or, to my taste even better, Kahlua. How right you are!

1 x Dark Chocolate Ice Cream recipe without the brandy
1 teaspoon of instant coffee granules – crushed
2 tablespoons of coffee liqueur
5 tablespoons coffee syrup

~ When melting together the chocolate, condensed milk, cocoa and in the original recipe also add the coffee granules.
~ Whip the cream together with your chosen coffee liqueur.
~ Fold together the whipped cream and the melted chocolate mixture.

- Put the ice cream into your chosen container.
- Drizzle over the coffee syrup and swirl in slightly but not completely.
- Freeze

Chocolate-Chilli Ripple

The advantage of this ice cream is that although delicious it is not universally popular so you might not have to share. I am fortunate enough to hang about with a few delicate types who won't touch the stuff.

1 x Dark Chocolate Ice Cream recipe
5 tablespoons of chilli syrup – see page 89

- Fold the chilli syrup into the whipped cream together with the melted chocolate mixture.
- Freeze.

If there is syrup over and you need a bit more heat – have yourself a drizzle.

White Chocolate Chip Ice Cream

The vanilla syrup here both compliments the white chocolate flavour and helps ensure a good creamy texture. My partner, who is a Geordie lad, said that this ice cream tastes like a white chocolate Magnum (something he loves) which is praise indeed from a man who usually saves the accolade "alreet" for something truly wonderful.

200g/1⅔ cups coarsely chopped white chocolate
200g/⅔ cup condensed milk
500ml/2 cups double cream
80ml/⅓ cup vanilla syrup
40g/⅓ cup more coarsely chopped white chocolate

- Put the 200g/1⅔ cups white chocolate and the condensed milk into a bowl. Melt over simmering water in accordance with the instructions at the start of the chapter.
- Cool to room temp but no cooler as it will firm up quite a lot.
- Whip the cream as usual and fold in the chocolate/condensed milk mixture.
- Fold in the vanilla syrup and the coarsely chopped white chocolate.
- Freeze.

White Chocolate & Coffee Ice Cream

This is the same as the above recipe but use coffee syrup instead of vanilla and leave out the coarsely chopped chocolate – unless you don't want to.

Chewy Double Chocolate Ripple

This was a pleasant surprise. When I made this chocolate sauce I was not sure about it, whilst deeply chocolatey, it is very thick and sticky when cold. Once swirled into the ice cream and frozen I found this to be an advantage – the sauce becomes thick and chewy and delicious.

1 batch White Chocolate Ice Cream - above
1 batch Sticky Chocolate Sauce (see page 78) – very slightly warmed for ease of rippling

~ Make the basic White Chocolate Ice Cream.
~ Ripple through with the chocolate sauce.
~ Freeze.

~ *Specifically Alcoholic Ice Creams* ~

Alcohol is often a good idea in ice cream, and not only for the obvious reason.

A little of an appropriate beverage (perhaps not brown ale, for instance) can really enhance an ice cream but too much and it will never freeze – you'll have to drink it. Heart-breaking! As I have already said elsewhere ideally add 50ml/3 tablespoons of spirit or liqueur per 500ml/2 cups cream. Wine is not strong enough to use neat and must be substantially reduced to a syrup before adding to the recipe and although it does make a reasonable ice cream it does seem a bit rude to the wine. For a better way to make wine syrup see the chapter on Sauces and Syrups, page 77.

I do think it is a kindness to say if alcohol is in a dish; not mentioning it could cause big problems for some people. It is pretty well true to say that in recipes in which the alcohol is cooked it will no longer be alcoholic having mostly evaporated off just leaving its yummy vital essence and its useful sugariness, but I would still mention it. Uncooked alcohol in ice cream can still make you pissed.

Whilst writing this book I was cooking in the pub down the road which was very useful to me. Whenever I needed a particular spirit or liqueur for a recipe I was testing I just had to buy a measure or two rather than a whole bottle. If you don't have a convenient well stocked bar to hand I find that brandy will stand in for almost anything! Story of my life, actually.

Brandied Cherry & White Chocolate Ice Cream

The dried cherries, having soaked up the alcohol, become juicy and squidgy and remain juicy and squidgy even in the midst of the sweet cold creaminess.

500ml/2 cups double cream
200g/⅔ cup condensed milk
40g/⅓ cup coarsely chopped white chocolate
225g/1½ cups dried cherries
brandy or cherry brandy to cover the cherries

~ At least 24 hours in advance of making this ice cream you must soak the cherries; put them into a small container and pour over enough brandy or cherry brandy to cover them. I can't give exact quantities but too much brandy is not a problem really, it will still be delicious after the cherries have been removed from it.
~ Melt the chocolate as instructed on page 44.
~ Whisk the cream together with 50ml/3 tablespoons of liquor drained from the soaking cherries.
~ Fold in the melted chocolate, condensed milk and macerated cherries.
~ Freeze.

Rum & Raisin (d'être) ~ I had to say that

This ice cream needs a few days forethought the first time you make it so you can macerate the fruit. Put dried fruit or just raisins, if you're going to be pedantic, into a jam jar and pour in enough golden rum to completely cover. I say rum because this is Rum and Raisin ice cream, but brandy is good too. I haven't given quantities here as you can do as much as you like. The fruit keeps almost forever provided you make sure it is always covered with alcohol and can be used it in all sorts of ways. You must, however, leave it alone for at least 24 hours.

500ml/2 cups double cream
200g/⅔ cup condensed milk
3 tablespoons of rum – preferably from rum soaked fruit jar as this has a lovely fruit infused flavour
225g/1½ cups rum soaked raisins

- ~ Whisk the double cream together with the rum till really thick.
- ~ Fold in the condensed milk and the raisins.
- ~ Freeze.

EITHER top up rum and/or fruit for another time OR relax and finish up the contents of the jar.

In direct contradiction to my father's edict that I should not play with my food I tried replacing the raisins in the above recipe with dried pineapple which I soaked in rum for a few days and then coarsely chopped. It was slightly crunchy, very alcoholic and not at all unpleasant.

Prune & Armagnac

This makes a rich, dark, alcoholic ice cream which is probably the nicest laxative you will ever taste, and which is extra good with a dark chocolate sauce.

170g/1¼ cups coarsely chopped prunes – *not* ready to eat
60ml/¼ cup Armagnac (or substitute Cognac if that is easier for you)
15g/1 tablespoon light brown sugar
500ml/2 cups double cream
200g/⅔ cup condensed milk

- ~ In a small pan over low heat warm together the Armagnac and the sugar, stirring till the sugar has dissolved. Add the prunes, cover and set aside off the heat for an hour or so.
- ~ Purée the prune mixture.
- ~ Whip the cream till thick.
- ~ Fold in the condensed milk.
- ~ Fold in the prune purée.
- ~ Freeze.

Amaretti-Amaretto

The crunchy sugary amaretti are a lovely contrast to the rich smooth alcoholic cream.

500ml/2 cups double cream
3 tablespoons Amaretto liqueur
approx. 40 Amaretti - little macaroon-ish biscuits
200g/⅔ cup condensed milk

- ~ Whisk the Amaretto together with the cream till thick.
- ~ Crush the Amaretti (maybe keeping back a few whole ones to serve alongside the ice cream in a sophisticated manner) and fold in together with the condensed milk.
- ~ Freeze.

Bramley Apple & Cider Ice Cream

This ice cream came about as a result of my working at the aforementioned pub. I started making homemade apple sauce for the Sunday Roasts using a delicious local cider; Cornish Rattler. It was a small progression, really, to just fold some of the apple sauce into my basic ice cream recipe, much to the delight of all the lads working in the pub. I can't remember that we actually sold any of the ice cream as it always mysteriously disappeared – I don't think they understood, bless'em, that cooking the cider evaporated off most of the alcohol.

500ml/2 cups double cream
200g/⅔ cup condensed milk
1 batch cold Apple Cider Sauce – page 80

- ~ Whip the cream till thick.
- ~ Fold in the condensed milk and the apple sauce.
- ~ Freeze.

Try making the same recipe with pears and perry (pear cider).

Painkiller Ice Cream!

I am not talking Aspirin or Paracetamol here. For a couple of years I was Executive Chef at Marina Cay, a beautiful little island resort in the West Indies owned by Pusser's Rum who have a chain of restaurants out there. The "house drink" is a Painkiller; a delicious pineapple, orange, coconut and rum punch based on an original drink devised by the Soggy Dollar Bar in Jost van Dyke, another small island in the British Virgins.

You may notice that this has quite a lot of alcohol in it. Rum is so plentiful in the islands that if you order a rum & coke and don't specify 'weak' you may well get a tumbler full of ice with say 80% rum to 20% coke, rum being the cheapest. If you do order 'weak' it might be 50:50 and if you ask for no ice well … brace yourself!

>1 batch Vastly Improved Desiccated Coconut – page 93
>3 tablespoons dark rum
>600g/2 cups pineapple chunked, fresh or canned in juice
>the flesh and finely grated zest of 4 oranges (no pith, no connective membrane)
>150g/¾ cup sugar
>another 3 tablespoons dark rum!
>500ml/2 cups double cream
>200g/⅔ cup condensed milk

~ Stir together the coconut and the first 3 tablespoons of rum.
~ Coarsely chop the pineapple and orange flesh and purée together with the orange zest, the sugar and the second 3 tablespoons of rum.
~ Whisk the cream till thick.
~ Fold in the condensed milk, then the pineapple purée and then the rum soaked coconut.
~ Freeze.

If you leave out the orange this will be Pina Colada Ice Cream.

Ti Punch Ice Cream

I am very partial to 'ti Punch, a traditional drink from the French Caribbean; the 'ti is short for petit. This small drink is different from the general idea of rum punches; it is strong, sweet, sharp and delicious and even has a poem to tell how to make it;

> *"One of sour*
> *Two of sweet*
> *Three of strong*
> *Four of weak"*

Sour is usually lime juice, sweet is sugar syrup or cane syrup (Golden Syrup for instance), strong is rum and weak is water but the last line is not strictly adhered to, if at all! The flavour of this ice cream reminds me of 'ti punch. There are quite a few spiced rums on the market but if you only have the normal un-spiced kind use that instead, not quite so exotic but still very pleasant.

500ml/2 cups double cream
100g/½ cup soft light brown sugar
finely grated zest and the juice of six lovely juicy limes
200g/⅔ cup condensed milk
3 tablespoons spiced rum

~ Mix together the cream and the sugar in a small pan and bring to just under the boil, stirring till the sugar has dissolved.
~ Simmer for 3 minutes.
~ Remove from the heat and whisk in the lime zest and juice which will cause the cream to thicken.
~ Set aside to cool and then chill till completely cold.
~ Add the rum, whisk till thick and fold in the condensed milk.
~ Freeze.

Buttered Rum & Ginger Ice Cream

5g/½ stick butter
55g/⅓ cup soft light brown sugar,
2 tablespoons of syrup from the stem ginger jar, coarsely chopped
3 tablespoons golden or dark rum
5 pieces of stem ginger – finely chopped
500ml/2 cups double cream
200g/⅔ cup condensed milk

- ~ Put the butter, sugar, ginger syrup and rum in a small pan and heat together over low heat stirring till everything has melted together
- ~ Stir in the chopped ginger and simmer gently for 3 or 4 minutes.
- ~ Cool completely.
- ~ Whisk the cream till thick.
- ~ Fold in the condensed milk.
- ~ Fold in the ginger and its sauce.
- ~ Freeze.

Baileys Ice Cream

Baileys is not as alcoholic as neat spirits or liqueurs being only 17% alcohol by volume compared to 34-40%, so I have used a little over double the usual amount.

500ml/2 cups double cream
200g/⅔ cup condensed milk
115ml/½ cup Baileys Irish Cream Liqueur

- ~ Whisk the Baileys together with the cream till thick.
- ~ Fold in the condensed milk.
- ~ Freeze.

Honey Mead Ice Cream

Many years ago, in our restaurant in Cornwall, we had an arrangement with an artist friend of ours. He would decorate our restaurant free of charge so long as we gave him such a free hand that he would come in at night and do surprising and delightful things whilst we slept! He hung a painting above our fireplace of two monks getting very drunk over a bottle of mead. There was candlelight on their faces and he insisted we always lit a candle at one and of the mantelpiece so that it looked as if it was actually throwing the light. He called it The Mead Louts.

This is delicious, but also difficult to identify, perhaps mead is an unfamiliar flavour.

340ml/1½ cups honey Mead
4 teaspoons of runny honey
500ml/2 cups double cream
200g/⅔ cup condensed milk – preferably the dulce de leche variety

~ Put the mead into a small non-reactive pan and boil till it has reduced by two thirds. Set aside to cool completely.
~ Whisk together the honey and cream (and dulce de leche if using) and as it thickens slowly whisk in the reduced mead till thick.
~ Fold in the condensed milk, if that is your preference.
~ Freeze.

Neat Spirit and Liqueur Ice Creams

Naturally I have tried whisking neat rum, bourbon, cognac etc. into the cream in the basic recipe but it wasn't very good. Bravely I soldiered on and found that the way to go is to use the appropriate syrup – see page 87 – which makes a beautifully creamy deliciously alcoholic ice cream and some liqueurs are excellent for this.

However, if all else fails just pour your favourite drink over your favourite ice cream!

~ Cakes, Biscuits, Meringues & Similar Additions ~

Adding inclusions can be both a great opportunity for creativity and a useful way to use up bits and pieces without being seen to do so.

These first two ice creams are all about inclusions and I thought they were cast-in-stone classics (especially Rocky Road – tee hee) but research has revealed that the recipes are just guidelines. There are certain requirements but within these bounds you can really go for it.

Tutti Frutti

Tutti Frutti means "all fruits" which gives a fair bit of scope. I have read about, seen and eaten Tutti Frutti Ice Creams containing … raisins, sultanas, dried cherries, mixed peel, cranberries, papaya, mango, apricots, crystallised ginger, pineapple, glacé cherries, dates, angelica, fresh banana, strawberries, peaches, almonds, hazelnuts, pecans, pistachios, coconut, mixed nuts, chocolate chips and probably other stuff too. The ice cream base has been vanilla, various fruit bases and, sometimes ices flavoured with a liqueur such as Kirsch, Cointreau or Brandy. The test recipe I "devised" for this book contained both roasted and crystallised pineapple, dried cranberries, glacé cherries, mixed peel and a bit of flaked coconut or, to put it another way, whatever appropriate I could find in the cupboard. My two favourite ice cream bases for Tutti Frutti are vanilla and Cointreau.

> 500ml/2 cups double cream
> 200g/⅔ cup condensed milk
> 80ml/⅓ cup vanilla syrup OR 3 tablespoons Cointreau
> approx. 400g/14 oz of your choice from all the additions listed above or anything else within reason – all coarsely chopped to a similar size

~ Whisk the cream and the Cointreau if using till thick.
~ Fold in the condensed milk and the vanilla syrup if using.
~ Fold in all your chosen inclusions.
~ Freeze.

Rocky Road

Rocky Road is less promiscuous than Tutti Frutti. Basically it is chocolate ice cream with mini marshmallows and nuts in it – an idea apparently thought up by an ice cream entrepreneur during the Great Depression to cheer people up! He originally used walnuts quickly changing to roasted almonds but subsequent recipes have contained, hazelnuts, pecans and peanut brittle. Chocolate chips or chopped up chocolate bars are sometimes included and, occasionally, fruit such as dried cherries, orange zest, etc. I like pecans, dark and white choc chips together with the obligatory marshmallows.

200g/⅔ cup condensed milk
180g/1½ cups coarsely chopped dark chocolate
1 tablespoon cocoa
500ml/2 cups double cream
approximately 275g/10 oz of chosen additions all coarsely chopped to a similar size

~ Put the condensed milk, the chocolate and the cocoa into a small bowl.
~ Stand the bowl in a few centimetres simmering water till the chocolate has melted and then stir together. This will be quite a thick mixture.
~ Cool slightly but not too much as it needs to be soft enough to fold into the cream.
~ Whip the cream till a little thickened. Add the chocolate goo and whisk till thick.
~ Fold in your selection of nuts, chocolate, marshmallows etc.
~ Freeze.

Elevensies Ice Cream

I spent a winter as pastry chef in the kitchen of a friend's very busy island restaurant. I made sugar cookies, as you do, to go with some of the desserts. Every night in the terrible scramble and rush of service, the poor wait-staff accidentally ate quite a lot of them. With the few broken cookies that were left I cunningly devised this ice cream.

There is a recipe for coffee syrup on page 87 and shortbread or the Danish butter cookies you can buy in a tin, quite cheaply are excellent for this recipe. Other broken biscuits you might have lying about will also work, of course, but do try to be sensible about it. I myself don't fancy garibaldi, for instance, but then I never did.

500ml/2 cups double cream
200g/⅔ cup condensed milk
1 teaspoon vanilla extract
as many broken biscuits as you can muster, within reason
150ml/⅔ cup coffee syrup plus extra for drizzling when serving

~ Whisk vanilla extract together with cream.
~ Fold in the condensed milk and the broken biscuits.
~ Partially fold in the coffee syrup to achieve a ripple effect.
~ Freeze.

Chocolate Ginger Crunch

180g/1½ cups coarsely chopped dark chocolate
30g/¼ cup cocoa
30g/2 tablespoons butter
200g/⅔ cup condensed milk
500ml/2 cups double cream
3 tablespoons ginger wine or, of course, brandy
2 knobs ginger from a jar of ginger in syrup – chopped
2 tablespoons ginger syrup
about 8 ginger snaps – crumbled

~   Put the chocolate into a small bowl together with the cocoa, the butter and the condensed milk.
~   Put the bowl in a small pan of boiling water so that the water comes about a third of the way up the bowl. If your bowl is plastic, it is a good idea to stand it on a metal jam jar lid or similar to stop it sticking to the bottom of the pan.
~   Simmer the water and stir the chocolate until it has melted into the condensed milk. This will be quite a thick mixture.
~   Cool slightly but not too much as it needs to be soft enough to fold into the cream.
~   Whip together the cream and the ginger wine or brandy.
~   Fold in the melted chocolate mixture, the ginger snaps, the ginger syrup and the chopped ginger.
~   Freeze.

This is particularly toothsome if you also ripple through a dark chocolate sauce before freezing.

Brown Bread Ice Cream

This ice cream, records of which can be found as early as 1772, and the two following are best served within a day or two so that the crunchy crumbs are still crunchy. After that the ice creams still taste delish but lack the texture.

225g/4 cups freshly crumbled brown bread crumbs
255g/1½ cups sugar
500ml/2 cups double cream
200g/⅔ cup condensed milk
1 teaspoon pure vanilla extract
good sloosh (remember a standard sloosh is about 50ml/3 tablespoons) brandy

~ Preheat oven to 180°C/350°F/160°C fan/gas 4.
~ On a baking sheet toss together the breadcrumbs and the sugar.
~ Put into the oven and bake, stirring frequently, till crisp and caramelised. Watch very carefully; it goes really quickly at the end. It will take about 10 minutes.
~ Cool, breaking up clumps if necessary.
~ Whisk the cream together with the vanilla extract and brandy till thick.
~ Fold the caramelised crumbs into the cream together with the condensed milk.
~ Freeze.

Shortly after making this I had an inspiration …

Hot Cross Bun Ice Cream

Just replace the brown bread crumbs with an equal quantity of crumbled up hot cross buns. I have to say – this is wonderful!

… and then another one …

Cinnamon Toast Ice Cream

This is very similar to the Brown Bread Ice Cream with just a few twists.

500ml/2 cups double cream
1 cinnamon stick broken into 3 or 4 pieces
60g/½ stick butter – melted
1½ level teaspoons of ground cinnamon
225g/4 cups freshly crumbled brown bread crumbs
255g/1½ cups light brown sugar
200g/⅔ cup condensed milk
80ml/⅓ cup vanilla syrup

- ~ Put the cinnamon pieces and the cream into a small pan and heat to just below boiling, turn off the heat, cover the pan and leave till cold. Remove the cinnamon sticks and chill the cream till completely cold.
- ~ Meanwhile, as they say in cookbooks, preheat the oven to 180ºC/350ºF/160ºC fan/gas 4.
- ~ Mix together the breadcrumbs, melted butter, sugar and ground cinnamon till all coated with butter.
- ~ Spread on a sheet pan and bake in the oven for about 10 minutes, stirring occasionally, till all golden brown and crisp.
- ~ When the cream is completely cold whisk it till thick.
- ~ Fold in the condensed milk and the vanilla syrup.
- ~ Fold in the crispy buttery crumbs.
- ~ Freeze.

Eton Mess & other Ice Cream & Meringue Combos

Meringues make a lovely addition to fruity ice creams. Crush them by squeezing or breaking till you have lumps to your liking and fold as much as you like, within reason, into the cream together with the condensed milk. If you use strawberries you could, quite rightly, call it Eton Mess Ice Cream or, with any fruit, Pavlova Ice Cream seems a suitable title – I am thinking about menu writing, you understand. You can, of course, use bought in meringues or there is a very easy fail proof recipe on page 94.

Peach & Brown Sugar Meringue Ice Cream

Add crushed Brown Sugar Meringues (page 95) to Peaches and Cream Ice Cream (page 28).

Coffee, Kahlua & Squidgy Chocolate Meringue Ice Cream

When I mentioned "luscious" in the title of this book I think I may have had this in mind. It's gorgeous! Based on Dark Chocolate Ice Cream (page 44) replace the "optional" brandy with 3 tablespoons of Kahlua and fold in crumbled Squidgy Chocolate Meringues (page 95).

Chocolate Brownie Caramel Swirl

May I recommend using a brownie with lumps of chocolate in it?

1 batch Dark Chocolate Ice Cream – see page 44
450g/1lb of the best chocolate brownies you can make or buy
1x 397g/14 oz can dulce de leche condensed milk

~ Make the chocolate ice cream.
~ Break the brownies into big crumbs or small lumps – about 1cm/½" pieces.
~ Fold the brownies into the ice cream.
~ Put the ice cream into your chosen container.
~ Gently spoon the dulce de leche on top of the ice cream. Swirl about a bit with a tea knife or similar so that you get little pockets and ripples of caramel in the ice cream.
~ Freeze.

Stracciatella Ice Cream

Stracciatella, in the ice cream world, are sort of posh chocolate chips; fragile shards and wisps of chocolate which are less intrusive and much more delicious than lumps.

1 batch ice cream of your choice ready to freeze
150g/1¼ cups coarsely chopped chocolate, also of your choice – but no rubbish, please

- Partially freeze the ice cream.
- After 45 minutes or so melt the chocolate over simmering water in accordance with the guidelines on page 44.
- Carefully pour the melted chocolate into a small sandwich bag. This is easy to do if you open the bag and insert it, open side up of course, into a small cup or glass. Fold the open edges down over the side of the glass and then you can pour in the chocolate with ease.
- Encourage all the chocolate into one corner.
- Get the semi frozen ice cream out of the freezer.
- Cut a tiny piece off the corner of the bag and squeeze the melted chocolate in a drizzly pattern over the semi frozen ice cream.
- As the melted chocolate hits the cold ice cream it immediately hardens into crisp little strips. Once it has done this stir them in a bit.
- Finish freezing the ice cream.

As with rippling serving this should further break up the chocolate pieces and disperse them amongst the ice cream.

Incidentally you could cheat and crumble a Flake into ice cream before freezing.

Honeycomb Ice Cream

I was mystified in New Zealand to see hokey pokey for sale, bought some, found it was honeycomb with a strange name and thought "hmm - Maori?" Then I remembered that my Mummy had mentioned hokey-pokey when I was little despite there being nothing antipodean about her. Hokey Pokey is also sometimes called cinder toffee, sponge toffee in Canada and yellowman in Ireland.

Fold a handful of crushed honeycomb (or a crumbled Crunchie bar!) into Honey (page 10) or Double Vanilla Ice Cream (page 19).

Fudge Crumble OR, perhaps, Scottish Tablet Ice Cream

The character of this ice cream depends entirely, of course, on your fudge. In Cornwall we are lucky enough to have access to Granny Wobbly's Fudge Pantry which sells, among other things, particularly gorgeous crumbly vanilla fudge which is similar to wonderful, wonderful Scottish Tablet (so much for being dour, by the way!).

Fold about 225g/8 oz of coarsely chopped fudge into a suitably flavoured ice cream such as chocolate, vanilla, banana and so forth.

Boodle-ish Orange Fool Ice Cream

Boodle's is a gentlemen's club which was founded in London in 1762 as a place where its members could "talk politics and play cards". Also eat, I believe, if their delicious orange fool is anything to go by. This luscious dessert has been a speciality on the menu for many years; apparently it started out as gooseberry fool but is now made with oranges and lemons which, to my mind, is probably an improvement. It is a sort of trifle/posset cross with foolish tendencies! Having made the fool for years I decided to branch out and make an ice cream version.

Using the recipe for Lemon Posset Ice Cream (page 22) replace three of the lemons with two oranges and fold in a couple of handfuls of broken sponge fingers or orange or lemon cake together with the condensed milk.

Alcoholic by Necessity Trifle Ice Cream

As opposed to ice cream trifle.

Alcohol is necessary to soak the fruit so it doesn't freeze solid in the ice cream. Sherry is traditional for trifle, but you need a spirit for the fruit so may I suggest … brandy? The sherry can be used in the cream. Don't eat and drive.

>410g-ish/14 oz-ish tin of fruit in juice
>3 tablespoons brandy or other suitable liqueur
>200g/7 oz trifle sponges or other plain cake - crumbled
>3 tablespoons sweet sherry
>500ml/2 cups double cream
>200g/⅔ cup condensed milk

~ Drain the fruit and discard or drink the juice.
~ Toss together the fruit and brandy or other liqueur and set aside overnight to soak.
~ The next day mix in the sponge cake.
~ Whisk the sherry and cream till thick.
~ Fold in the condensed milk and then the fruit, sponge and alcohol mixture.
~ Freeze.

Apart from the above recipe, I generally use a variation of the syrup method to add cake to an ice cream base. I flavour the syrup with ingredients which compliment or, maybe, mirror those of the cake I am using and then I crumble some of the cake into the syrup.

Christmas Pudding Ice Cream

Recently I have seen a lot of different recipes for Christmas Pudding Ice Cream, but this is the version I have been using for years. It is one of my most asked for recipes, although admittedly most of the requests are from my friend Clarky who is a forgetful sort of a chap.

225g/8 oz cooked Christmas Pud
30g/2 tablespoons butter
30g/2 tablespoons dark brown sugar
finely grated zest and juice of 1 orange
3 tablespoons brandy
500ml/2 cups double cream
200g/⅔ cup condensed milk

~ Crumble the Christmas pudding with your fingers.
~ Lick fingers.
~ Wash fingers.
~ Melt together the butter and the sugar and then stir in the crumbled pud, the orange juice and zest and the brandy.
~ Bring slowly to a simmer, stirring a lot, and then cool completely.
~ Whisk the cream till thick.
~ Fold in the pudding mixture together with condensed milk.
~ Freeze.

Treacle Pudding Ice Cream

Isn't it strange how everyone calls Golden Syrup 'treacle'? Me too.

6 tablespoons Golden Syrup
225g/8 oz crumbled sponge cake – ideally Golden Syrup cake.
500ml/2 cups double cream
200g/⅔ cup condensed milk

~ Gently warm the syrup and stir in the crumbled cake.
~ Cool completely.
~ Fold into the whipped cream together with the condensed milk.
~ Freeze.

This is attractive frozen in individual bombes, turned out and topped with a spoonful of Golden Syrup like little frozen Treacle Puds.

Carrot Cake Ice Cream

30g/2 tablespoons butter
30g/2 tablespoons light brown sugar,
finely grated zest and juice of 1 orange
225g/8 oz carrot cake - crumbled
500ml/2 cups double cream
200g/⅔ cup condensed milk
maybe some toasted pecans or walnuts – see page 92

~ Gently melt together the butter and sugar.
~ Stir in the orange zest and juice and the crumbled cake.
~ Cool completely.
~ Whip the cream and fold in the condensed milk, the cake mixture and nuts, if using.
~ Freeze.

Banana Rum Cake Ice Cream

80ml/⅓ cup rum syrup – page 87
225g/8 oz banana cake – crumbled
1 batch Rum Roasted Banana Ice Cream (page 33) – ready to freeze

~ Warm together the cake and the syrup and then cool again.
~ Fold into the Rum Roasted Banana Ice Cream.
~ Freeze.

Jamaican Gingerbread Ice Cream

4 tablespoons ginger syrup from stem ginger jar
60ml/¼ cup dark rum
3 or 4 pieces of ginger from the same jar – finely chopped
225g/8 oz Jamaican gingerbread or similar cake
500ml/2 cups double cream
200g/⅔ cup condensed milk

~ Gently heat together the syrup and rum.
~ Add the chopped ginger and crumbled cake.
~ Cool.
~ Fold into the whipped cream together with the condensed milk.
~ Freeze.

Sticky Toffee Pudding Ice Cream

I think you must be getting the gist by now! Warm some Sticky Toffee Sauce (page 79) crumble in 225g/8 oz Sticky Toffee Pudding and when cold fold it into the whipped cream together with the condensed milk.

~ *Savoury, Interesting & Peculiar* ~

One of the few strange things about Americans is their use of the term "a la mode". I have always understood this to be French for "in the manner/style/fashion", perhaps a way of doing things particular to a certain restaurant. Discombobulatingly enough in America it means served with ice cream – I would have thought that if, for some reason, you wanted to say "with ice cream" in French then something like 'avec crème glacé' would have done the trick.

Once in the Caribbean, where there are a lot of American chaps, for pure divilment I put 'Home Smoked Seafood Platter a la mode' on the menu and watched the funny reactions (I had an open kitchen). I served the seafood with a Vodka, Lemon and Parsley Ice Cream and I wish I could give the recipe here but I can't for two good reasons. Firstly the savoury nature of the dish doesn't lend itself to this method using, as it does, so much sweet condensed milk and, secondly, I have no idea how I did it – probably in an ice cream machine.

My creativity, however, comes nowhere near that of the ice cream shop Heladeria Coromoto in Merida, Venezuela which sells 860+ flavours including gherkin, spaghetti and cheese, horseradish, brandied sardines and Viagra! Nor does it approach that of Gino Soldan, a master gelatiera who created a range of 20 ice creams based on traditional British foods for a special promotion in Harrods a few years ago. The flavours included Worcestershire Sauce, Haggis, Arbroath Smokie and Stottie Cake.

Strawberry Balsamic Ripple

I have been making a balsamic vinegar and honey glaze for many a long year; at work drizzling it on plates as a fancy garnish, at home putting it on hummus, risotto, salad, etc. It has become a kind of posh ketchup for me. It's easy enough to make but fills your kitchen with vinegary fumes and this can be avoided nowadays by simply buying a bottle of the stuff in the supermarket. I tried adding a swirl of this to basic strawberry ice cream and wasn't very impressed so I left it sat sitting in the freezer for a week or so, forgotten and forlorn. When I tried it again I had changed my mind. I really liked the sweet/sharp syrupy tang rippling through the bright strawberry flavour. Try it – just ripple balsamic glaze though a batch of Strawberry Ice Cream (page 27) before freezing.

I also tried adding, as one does, a good grinding of black pepper and it was pleasant enough, nothing wrong with it at all but I think I would prefer just to grind the pepper freshly over the ice cream as I ate it. Even better is to serve fresh strawberries with this …

Cracked Black Pepper Ice Cream

This quantity of syrup makes an ice cream that is, at first, just a pleasant vanilla flavour but which after a time takes on a certain warmth. If you like a lot of spiciness sprinkle with freshly ground black pepper to serve.

500ml/2 cups double cream
200g/⅔ cup condensed milk
3 tablespoons brandy
1 teaspoon pure vanilla extract
80ml/⅓ cup black pepper syrup – page 85

~ Whisk together the cream, the brandy and the vanilla extract.
~ Fold in the condensed milk and the black pepper syrup.
~ Freeze.

Werther's Original Crunch – and beyond?

This started out as a silly idea but worked really well, so here's the recipe.

500ml/2 cups double cream
200g/⅔ cup condensed milk – dulce de leche style is best
1 batch sticky toffee sauce
200g/7 oz Werther's Originals

~ Using a pestle and mortar crush the Werther's Originals into small-ish crumbs.
~ Whip the cream and dulce de leche (if using) till thick.
~ Fold in the condensed milk (if using that instead) and then the toffee sauce and finally the crushed Werther's Originals.
~ Freeze.

It could get sillier – how about, using the same method, a Tunes ice cream, maybe ripple through with the merest touch of cough medicine (don't overdose!), or perhaps something using a Fisherman's Friend?

Popping Candy

Back in the 70s, popping candy was called space dust and our cat was called Mulberry. Sometimes Mulberry and I shared some space dust; I'd put a few grains on his tongue and he'd immediately run around the room with his tail straight up, as did I. After a minute or two he'd come and stand in front of me with his tongue out waiting for more. My love interest is less adventurous than the cat and, at 48 years old, claims to have never tried the stuff. I bought him a packet, but he spurned it so, as with most things these days, I wondered what it would be like in ice cream.

My research has revealed that popping candy dissolves in water and melts in heat but doesn't seem to be so affected by cold fatty goo. It does start popping when it is mixed in with the ice cream but so long as you add it just before freezing and immediately press some cling film over the surface, it's OK.

This isn't a recipe; just an idea for which I have three pieces of advice:

1. Work quickly so that the candy freezes before it gets too wet and pops.
2. Eat the ice cream quite soon for the same reason
3. Be careful what flavour you get – some of them are pretty chemical tasting although I understand they are just "normal hard candy" with carbon dioxide trapped into it.

Smoky Bacon and Maple Syrup Ice Cream

This flavour combination has made the news recently in part thanks to Heston Blumenthal but years ago, before I had heard of him (or he me!) I had been making this recipe for our busy Sunday brunches in Tortola. Also I believe "The Two Ronnies" mentioned something similar in 1973.

I have to say that American cream might be a bit second rate but their bacon is extremely good; similar to our streaky but to my mind much, much nicer! It must be the way that they cure it, when cooked it is crispy, salty, melting and delicious, especially when served like this.

Brush smoked streaky bacon rashers with maple syrup and cook on a baking tray under a hot grill to crisp. Cool and then sprinkle over or fold into Maple Syrup Ice Cream, the easiest recipe ever, on page 10.

Blue Cheese Ice Cream

Use a soft-ish blue cheese to make these ice creams; Dolcelatte is perfect and so is Saint Agur.

This is the basic recipe; if you add nothing else to it the ice cream will be firm-ish, but tasty. The variations that follow make a tasty blue cheese ice cream that is also rich and creamy.

200g/1¾ cups chosen blue cheese – crumbled
500ml/2 cups double cream
200g/⅔ cup condensed milk
3 tablespoons brandy

~ Break or crumble the blue cheese into a mixing bowl and add half the cream.
~ Whisk on medium/slow to mix the cheese and cream together.
~ Add the rest of the cream and the brandy.
~ Turn up the speed of the mixer and whisk till thick.
~ Fold in the condensed milk.
~ Freeze.

This is good with a drizzle of honey.

Blue cheese ice cream is very acceptable indeed served with hot baked pears, or try …

Blue Cheese and Baked Pear Ice Cream

In addition to the basic Blue Cheese Ice Cream recipe you will need …

1 batch Butterscotch Baked Pears – see ice cream of the same name on page 34

~ Fold the pears in with the condensed milk.
~ Freeze.

Blue Cheese & Port Ripple

In addition to the basic Blue Cheese Ice Cream recipe you will need …

80ml/⅓ cup Port Syrup – page 88

~ Fold half of the port syrup in with the condensed milk.
~ Decant into your chosen container and ripple in the other half.
~ Freeze

Peppered Blue Cheese Ice Cream

In addition to the basic Blue Cheese Ice Cream recipe you will need …

80ml/⅓ cup Black Pepper Syrup – page 85

~ Fold the syrup in with the condensed milk.
~ Freeze

Goats Cheese & Hazelnut Ice Cream

Something of this ilk was my first foray into unusual ice creams back in the 1980s and was even mentioned in the 1986 Good Food Guide entry for our restaurant where it was deemed to be "excellent". As with many things from when I was young I can't remember quite how I did it, so this isn't the same recipe. Still excellent though.

200g/¾ cup soft goat cheese
500ml/2 cups double cream
200g/⅔ cup condensed milk
80ml/⅓ cup bought in hazelnut syrup OR 3 tablespoons Frangelico Liqueur
100g/¾ cup toasted hazelnuts (page 92) – chopped

~ Gently whisk together the cheese and half the cream till soft and then add the rest of the cream and the liqueur if using.
~ Turn up the speed and whisk till thick.
~ Fold in the condensed milk and the syrup if using plus the nuts.
~ Freeze.

Peppered Goats Cheese Ice Cream

As above but replacing the hazelnut syrup with black pepper syrup (page 85) and leaving out the nuts.

Butternut Squash (or Pumpkin) and Maple Syrup Ice Cream

500g/3 cups 1cm/½" diced butternut squash (or pumpkin)
2 tablespoons maple syrup
30g/2 tablespoons soft light brown sugar
30g/2 tablespoons butter
pinch of sea salt
pinch of cinnamon
500ml/2 cups double cream
another 2 tablespoons of maple syrup
200g/⅔ cup condensed milk

~ Preheat the oven to 180°C/350°F/160°C fan/gas 4 and lightly grease a baking dish.
~ Gently melt together 2 tablespoons maple syrup, sugar, butter, salt and cinnamon, toss with the squash (or pumpkin) and add to the pan.
~ Cover with foil and bake for 30 minutes.
~ Remove the foil and continue to bake till completely tender and starting to caramelise.
~ Mash or purée and cool completely.
~ Whisk the cream till thick, fold in the squash (or pumpkin), the second 2 tablespoons of maple syrup and the condensed milk.
~ Freeze.

Toasted pecans (see page 92) or pumpkin seeds are good folded into this ice cream or make an appropriate brittle (see page 92 again!) to serve with it.

Roasted Beetroot and Chocolate Ice Cream

3 or 4 raw beetroot – weighing about 500g/18 oz
80ml/⅓ cup Dark Chocolate Caramel Sauce – page 76
500ml/2 cups double cream
200g/⅔ cup condensed milk

~ Preheat oven to 180ºC/350ºF/160ºC fan/gas 4.
~ Wash the beetroots and wrap in foil. Bake to totally tender – up to two hours.
~ Unwrap and peel whilst still warm which is easiest.
~ Purée the flesh together with the chocolate sauce and cool completely.
~ Whisk the cream till thick, fold in the purée and the condensed milk.
~ Freeze.

Black Garlic Ice Cream!

Black garlic is my favourite "new" ingredient in years; it is mellow, soft and sweet like a dried fruit version of garlic and as it has such a wonderful molasses-ish taste I decided rum would be the correct addition.

The first time I tried this I only made a modicum in case it was yuk but it was lovely!

500ml/2 cups double cream
200g/⅔ cup condensed milk
8 of the softest black garlic cloves you can muster
3 tablespoons rum

~ Purée the black garlic with 50ml/3 tablespoons of the cream.
~ Stir in the rest of the cream and the rum and whisk till thick.
~ Fold in the condensed milk.
~ Freeze.

~ Sauces, Syrups, Coulis & Curds ~

A sauce is an excellent way to dress up an ice cream. Of course, chocolate sauce immediately springs to mind but there are others you know.

Sticky Chocolate Sauce

The golden syrup (or you could use corn syrup) makes this sauce sticky when warm and chewy when very cold so is the one to use in Chewy Double Chocolate Ripple (page 48). This makes about 150ml/⅔ cup of sauce.

60g/½ cup coarsely chopped dark chocolate
100g/½ cup sugar
2 tablespoons of golden syrup
1 tablespoon cocoa
3 tablespoons water
½ teaspoon coffee granules - crushed
30g/2 tablespoons butter

~ Put everything except the butter into a small pan and heat gently till melted all together.
~ Stir over low heat for a few minutes, 4 or 5, till smooth and shiny.
~ Take off the heat and beat in the butter till melted and smooth.
~ Cool.

Serve hot over ice cream or anything you fancy.

Extreme Chocolate Sauce

This sauce, being cocoa based, is very rich and strong and is ideal for drizzling over dishes as a dark chocolate counterpoint. Makes about 150ml/⅔ cup of sauce.

80ml/⅓ cup double strength coffee
85g/½ cup soft dark brown sugar
50g/⅓ cup cocoa
30g/2 tablespoons butter
1 tsp vanilla extract

~ In a small pan over low heat stir together the sugar and the coffee till the sugar is completely dissolved.
~ Whisk in the cocoa till all smooth.
~ Add the butter and the vanilla extract and whisk again till the butter is melted and all mixed together.

Dark or Milk or White Chocolate Caramel Sauce

These sauces are all lovely although it would be difficult, I think, to beat the white chocolate version – it's just delish. This recipe makes about 250ml/1 cup of sauce.

100g/½ cup granulated sugar
60ml/¼ cup water
150ml/⅔ cup double cream
90g/¾ cup coarsely chopped dark, milk or white chocolate
pinch of salt
1 tsp vanilla extract

~ Set the cream beside the stove.
~ In a deep saucepan over low heat stir together the sugar and the water till the sugar is dissolved and then bring to a boil. Don't stir any more but when it begins turning golden you can swirl it about a bit to even out the colour.
~ Cook to a deep golden brown watching carefully and swirling occasionally.
~ When you are happy with the colour add the cream and stir over low heat till the caramel which will have hardened has melted back into the cream.
~ Add the chocolate and stir till completely melted and mixed into the sauce.
~ Add the salt and vanilla extract and stir in.

Sticky Toffee Sauce

Do not boil this sauce after adding the cream or else! In my first restaurant where we were very, very silly it was said that the penalty for boiling the Sticky Toffee Sauce was that it would be poured down your knickers.

120g/1 stick butter
250g/1½ cup soft dark brown sugar
1 teaspoon vanilla extract
175ml/¾ cup double cream

~ Melt together the butter and dark brown sugar, stirring all the time.
~ Add the vanilla essence and stir it in.
~ Add the cream and stir in completely, bring to a fast simmer but do not boil.
~ Cool.

Sticky Toffee Sauce keeps very well but sometimes, on reheating, the butter separates out. If this happens just add a little splash of cold cream and stir in. The sauce will immediately re-emulsify.

Apple Cider Sauce

This is also excellent served warm with roast pork!

5 Bramley apples
150g/¾ cup sugar (maybe a bit more depending on the apples)
300ml/1¼ cups cider

~ Bring the cider and the sugar to a boil, stirring till the sugar has dissolved.
~ Turn down a little to a slow boil or a rapid simmer and cook till a light golden syrup has occurred – this will take about 10 minutes. The syrup should be not quite caramelised but taking a little colour.
~ Meanwhile core and slice the apples.
~ When the cider is syrupy and golden add the apples and return to a boil.
~ Turn down the heat, cover the pan and cook for about 10 minutes stirring from time to time. The apples will naturally break down into a kind of chunky sauce which is why I recommend using Bramleys.
~ When all cooked and mushy beat with a wooden spoon to achieve your ideal apple sauce texture.

Caramel/Pineapple/Rum Sauce

I have made this with fresh pineapple but the difference in taste is minimal and the increase in labour is on the maximal side. Of course, if you've got a fresh pineapple lying about the place …

450g/2¼ cups granulated sugar
small can (227g/8 oz) pineapple in fruit juice
3 tablespoons rum or Malibu

~ Drain the pineapple setting aside the juices.
~ Coarsely chop the pineapple.
~ Put the fruit juice right beside the stove.
~ In a small heavy pan over medium heat stir together the sugar and 120ml/½ cup of water till the sugar is dissolved completely.

~ Turn up the heat and boil the sugar, watching it all the while but not stirring at all, but you can carefully swirl the pan a bit as it takes on colour.
~ Watch carefully.
~ As soon as it reaches a lovely rich golden-brown caramel colour carefully pour in the fruit juice. This will splatter a bit so stand back. Stir over the flame till the caramel, which will have hardened, melts again.
~ Stir in the chopped pineapple, turn down the heat and simmer for about 10 minutes till the pineapple is a little darker.
~ Away from the heat stir in the rum or Malibu.
~ Cool the sauce and then chill till needed.

Lemon/Orange/Lime Curd

When a recipe calls for the zest of fruits it is so much easier if you grate it from the fruits before squeezing out the juice.

3 large eggs
finely grated zest and freshly squeezed juice of 2-3 lemons (or 4-5 limes or maybe just 1 or 2 oranges or even a combination) to amount to 80ml/⅓ cup
150g/¾ cup sugar
60g/½ stick room temperature butter in small pieces

~ Put a nylon strainer over a bowl beside the stove.
~ Break the eggs into a mixing bowl and beat in the citrus juice and the sugar.
~ Stand the mixing bowl in a small pan containing a little boiling water.
~ Cook over medium heat, stirring absolutely constantly, until the mixture starts to thicken. This will take a while, maybe 10 minutes or so and, if you have such a thing as a sugar thermometer you are aiming 160°F/71°C
~ Strain immediately.
~ Whisk in the butter pieces and the zest.
~ Cool, press cling film on the surface to stop a skin forming and chill.

Raspberry Curd

340g/1½ cups fresh raspberries
200g/1 cup sugar
4 tablespoons lemon juice
60g/½ stick butter
good pinch salt
4 eggs

~ Put a nylon strainer over a bowl beside the stove.
~ In a small non-stick pan heat together all the ingredients except the eggs, whisking till smooth and the sugar has melted.
~ In a separate bowl whisk the eggs together till well blended.
~ Pour a little of the hot raspberry goo into the eggs, whisking constantly (this is known as tempering – a lot of things are!).
~ Pour the egg and raspberry mixture back into the pan and stir into the hot raspberry mixture.
~ Cook over medium heat, stirring absolutely constantly, until the mixture starts to thicken but Be Careful – if it gets too hot you will have raspberry sauce with scrambled eggs in it.
~ As soon as it thickens pour through the strainer.
~ Chill till needed.

Fresh Fruit Sauces, Purées and Coulis(es?)

Originally the word coulis referred to "the juices that flow from meat when cooking" but these days it is just a posh word for fruit purée. It is up to you whether to strain the purée or not although I must warn you that the word "coulis" is also said to come from the Latin verb to strain, so it may depend on how pedantic you are. With pippy fruits such as blackberries and raspberries it is probably a good idea. Fruit coulis can be made from almost any fruit, including tomatoes with appropriate flavourings, but soft summer fruits are the go for me.

fresh summer fruits (de-stalked, topped and tailed, washed, etc.)
sugar (approximately half the weight of the fruit)

Either …

~ Put the prepared fruit in a small saucepan.
~ Add the sugar to the fruit.
~ Simmer, helpfully giving the fruit a squash now and then – you could add a dribble of water to encourage the sugar to melt if the fruit isn't very juicy.
~ Strain through a fine nylon sieve pushing on the fruit debris to extract as much coulis as poss.
~ Cool, cover and chill till needed.

Or …

~ Put the prepared fruit a liquidizer or food processor.
~ Add the sugar to the fruit and purée together.
~ Cover and keep cool till needed.

Syrups and Crystallised Fruits

I have included crystallised fruits under this heading because the method of crystallising produces a delicious syrup as by-product.

Syrups are useful for all sorts of things in addition to making ice cream. Use as a cordial, topping up with sparkling water, lemonade or Champagne, add to fruit salad or try lightly poaching fruits the syrup. Pour over ice cream sundaes and other desserts. Add to cocktails. Brush over fruit tarts or cake tops as a glaze or brush on all layers of a layer cake for added moistness and flavour. If you pour hot syrup over a hot cake (fresh out of the oven) it will be absorbed. Orange syrup soaked into carrot cake, for instance, is great.

Syrups are also essential for making sorbets and granitas – see the companion volume to this book; "*Sorbets and Granitas*" for lots of good ideas.

There are, however, a few things you should know and precautions you should take when making syrup.

~ Use a small-ish but deep pan as it may very well boil up, especially when making caramel based syrups.
~ I have read and been told over and over again that you should brush down the insides of the pan with a damp pastry brush to remove sugar crystals as not doing so will lead to grainy syrup. I have never found this to be true but maybe I'm just a freak of nature
~ Try not to splash yourself; this stuff is Very Hot, don't be tempted to stick your finger or any other part of your body into it and always stir with a wooden spoon as a metal one will get uncomfortable to hold, don't lick the spoon until the syrup has cooled down.
~ Let the syrup cool in the pan for a little while for any bubbles to settle down and to avoid melting the container.

~   If you are leaving in or adding any solid matter (herbs, spices etc.) make sure these are completely and utterly under the surface of the syrup at all times or they will go mouldy and ruin the whole batch.

Being mainly sugar and water, and sometimes alcohol, these syrups keep very well. On returning to our caravan after a winter away I found half a squeezy bottle of coffee syrup in the corner of a cupboard, where I had left it the previous October. It was fine and a pleasant surprise.

Label assiduously, you may think you'll never forget what it is but you will, particularly when making cocktails. Store in the fridge or sometimes just in a cupboard depending on your location and the time of year. Obviously, syrups are thicker when cold and might need a little relaxation time at room temperature. They may even crystallise, especially if kept in the fridge, but no worries; just stand it in warm water for a few minutes.

The easiest and most pleasurable way to clean the pan after you have poured out your flavoured syrup is to add some water to the pan, bring to a boil, stirring with the wooden spoon to dissolve any residual syrup and to clean the spoon. Then make yourself a cup of coffee with the resulting flavoured water.

Basic Syrup Recipe

This is "simple syrup" which is used in many applications from cocktails to all the other uses listed above. If you just want to boost the lushness of an ice cream without interfering with the flavour this is the one for you!

> 250g/1¼ cup sugar
> 120ml/½ cup water

~   Put the water and sugar into a small pan and stir over medium low heat till the sugar has dissolved, brushing down the sides of the pan with damp brush, or not, depending on how freaky you feel (see above).
~   When the liquid is clear turn up the heat till it boils and then turn it down again to allow it to boil more slowly.
~   Boil gently till thick which takes about 5 minutes. During this stage of the proceedings, don't stir it but do pay attention.
~   The syrup is ready when it forms a thread if you drip a little off the spoon. If you have a sugar thermometer you are aiming for 223°-235°F which is 106°-112° C. I usually stop cooking at the lower temperature so that the syrup is still a bit runny when chilled.
~   When cool enough decant into an appropriate container.

The following recipes are all based on the above recipe for simple syrup.

Vanilla Syrup

~ Use a small sharp knife to slit two nice pliable vanilla pods lengthways.
~ Use the tip of the knife to scrape the tiny black seeds from the pods into the just melted sugar and water. Also add the pods and continue as above.
~ When finished you can either leave the vanilla pods in for a stronger taste or take them out, rinse and dry them and use them for something else.

Black Pepper Syrup

This looks a little bit like the vanilla syrup but the black dots are bigger – label carefully.

~ When the sugar has melted into the water add two tablespoons of coarsely ground black pepper – freshly ground if you can manage it
~ When ready strain the syrup and then stir a little of the pepper back in to taste and to look speckled, but not too much – I think you want the pepper heat and flavour to be background-ish.
~ Cool and chill till needed.

Ginger Syrup

No need to peel the ginger here unless the skin is manky. If you do want to peel it, however, be my guest – I find it easiest using the edge of a teaspoon which seems to scrape easily into all the ginger's nooks and crannies.

~ Add 50g/½ cup of thinly sliced fresh root ginger once the sugar has melted, return to the boil and then simmer for about 5 minutes till syrupy.
~ Cook a little longer than usual, to 235°F /112° C, because you then …
~ … stir in the juice of 1 lime which will, of course, dilute the syrup slightly.
~ Cool then strain or for a stronger taste leave the ginger in the syrup making sure that it is completely submerged or it may go mouldy.

Lavender Syrup

~ Add 2 teaspoons of dried lavender or 4 teaspoons of fresh lavender flowers once the sugar has melted, return to the boil and then simmer for about 5 minutes to syrupy.
~ Cool then strain.

You could add a few fresh lavender flowers to the syrup for prettiness and as an aide memoire in case your label falls off.

The following recipes are similar to the first few, but the syrup is caramelised

Caramel Syrup

250g/1¼ cup sugar
120ml/½ cup water
an additional 120ml/½ cup water

~ Set 120ml/½ cup of water beside the stove within easy reach.
~ Heat together the sugar and the other 120ml/½ cup water over medium heat, stirring it often, until sugar is dissolved, as above.
~ Don't stir any more but boil gently until it begins turning colour. At this stage you can carefully swirl the syrup about in the bottom of the pan to even out the colour.
~ Cook to a deep golden brown watching carefully and swirling occasionally.
~ As soon as it reaches golden brown, all at once yet carefully (it will boil rapidly) add the water you have placed beside the stove.
~ Cook gently stirring until the caramel, which will have hardened, has melted back into the syrup.
~ Cook till it is thick and syrupy as above.
~ Cool.

Brandy/Bourbon/Whisky/Rum etc. Syrup

250g/1¼ cup sugar
120ml/½ cup water
an additional 60ml/¼ cup water
120ml/½ cup chosen spirit

~   As above but when caramelising the syrup cook it to a lovely golden colour rather than a deep reddish brown – a Brandy/ Bourbon/Whisky/Rum colour, if you will.
~   You will notice you are adding less water at the end – once the caramel has melted into the water lift the pan and turn away from the heat. Add the spirit and stir in thoroughly.
~   Return to the heat and cook a few minutes till the syrup has thickened slightly.
~   Cool.

Coffee Syrup

I have added a pinch of salt to the coffee in this recipe. My father used to add a pinch of salt to coffee and for years I didn't understand why, although it did taste good. Now I am all grown up I realise that salt somehow reduces coffee's bitterness and enhances the flavour – "Good Girl Daddy" as I used to say before I became so mature, some weeks ago, now!

Double strength coffee is, of course, coffee made with twice as much coffee to water as you usually use (or half as much water to coffee, whichever you prefer!). I use a cafetière or French press with 4 tablespoons ground coffee. I pour over 300ml/1¼ cups almost but not quite boiling water and leave a few minutes before pressing the plunger. Remember the coffee will continue getting stronger even after plunging so pour when it tastes to your liking. Cool and then measure off 250ml/1¼ cups for the recipe.

250g/1¼ cup sugar
120ml/½ cup water
a pinch of salt
240ml/1 cup double strength coffee (see above)

~   Set the coffee beside the stove.
~   In a saucepan over low heat stir together the sugar and the water till the sugar is dissolved and then bring to a boil. Don't stir any more but when it starts turning colour you can swirl it about a bit.

~ Boil to a deep golden brown watching carefully, swirling occasionally.
~ As soon as it reaches deep golden brown all at once yet carefully (it will boil rapidly) add the coffee and stir over medium heat till the caramel has melted back into the coffee.
~ Add the pinch of salt.
~ Simmer stirring occasionally till the syrup has reduced and thickened slightly – about 5 minutes.
~ Cool.

Port or Red Wine Syrup

These are both good; wine is cheaper, port is richer

In addition to using in ice cream these two syrups are delicious drizzled over blue cheese.

~ Put equal quantities of port or red wine and sugar into a small deep pan and follow the basic method on page 84.
~ Cool.

Crystallised Orange & its Ensuing Syrup

You can mostly sit and read or watch telly or play online bingo or whatever whilst this is cooking but do check occasionally. What you are checking for is that the fruit juice has not reduced and thickened too much. If it is too thick and getting frothy add a splash of hot water. Remember you are aiming not only for tender zest but also a syrupy syrup – not jam.

2 gorgeous oranges

200g/1 cup white sugar
200g/1⅓ cup icing sugar

~ Wash and dry two lovely bright unblemished oranges.
~ Using a potato peeler peel long strips of zest from the fruit – just the bright orange skin, not the white and bitter pith underneath.

~ Using a sharp knife cut the zest into little strips, or "julienne".
~ Squeeze the juice from the denuded fruits into a measuring jug and, if necessary, make up to 500mll/2 cups with water.
~ Bring the juice and sugar to a boil stirring till the sugar has dissolved.
~ Add the orange zest strips, partly cover the pan and simmer very gently, topping up occasionally, till the zest is tender – 45-60 minutes.
~ Turn off the heat and cool a little in the pan.
~ Strain, keeping both the zest and the syrup.
~ Preheat oven to 140°C/275°F/120°C fan/gas 1.
~ Sift the icing sugar onto a baking sheet or large plate and roll the orange zest in the icing sugar to coat it.
~ Spread out on a non-stick pan liner or baking parchment and bake for an hour or so to dry out.
~ Cool and keep dry for up to 3 months.
~ Also keep the syrup.

Crystallised Chilli & its Syrup

A little of this syrup is delicious stirred into a tropical fruit salad and is absolutely wonderful in hot chocolate.

150g/¾ cup white sugar
300ml/1¼ cups water
150g/½ cup medium hot bright red chillies – seeded, white membrane removed and thinly sliced

~ Bring the sugar and the water to a boil, stirring to dissolve the sugar.
~ Add the chilli and cook on a low heat, topping up with a little water as necessary, for 45 minutes.
~ Preheat oven to 180°C/350°F/160°C fan/gas 4.
~ Strain the chillies into a bowl and set the syrup aside to cool.
~ Spread the chillies out on a non-stick pan liner of parchment and do in the oven for 20 - 25 minutes, stirring and separating as they dry, till beginning to crisp remembering that they will be crisper when cool.
~ When completely cold break up any that are clinging together and store in an airtight container.

~ *Inclusions, Complimentary Stuff & Ancillary Recipes* ~

Here are various recipes to help create, augment and serve the ice creams.

Caramel

Throughout the book are recipes containing caramel so here are a few guidelines and safety tips to help with this.

~ Use a wooden spoon so that it neither gets too hot nor melts.
~ Use a capacious pan so that the caramel has plenty of room.
~ If possible don't use a non-stick pan as they are too dark to see the colour of the caramel.
~ Equip yourself with a good heatproof cloth.
~ Put any additions immediately to hand beside the stove.
~ Never touch hot caramel with anything human or animal.

How to Make Caramel

You need to make caramel at least an hour or so before using it, depending on your location, to let it harden. Crushing is achieved either by using a sturdy pestle in a rough grained mortar or by wrapping it a tea towel and bashing the bejesus out of it with a hammer or something similar.

100g/½ cup white sugar
60ml/¼ cup water

~ Lightly grease a baking tray with something tasteless in the vegetable oil department and put it close to the stove, standing on a wooden board or folded cloth; it will get very hot when the caramel is pour onto it.
~ In a pan over low heat stir together the sugar and the water till the sugar is dissolved and then bring to a boil. Don't stir once it boils but swirl about a bit when it begins turning colour.
~ Boil to a deep golden brown *watching carefully*.
~ Immediately it reaches the right colour all at once yet carefully (because this is very hot and burny) pour the caramel onto the greased baking tray and tip the tray a little to make the caramel flow out thinly.
~ Leave to cool.
~ When the caramel is completely cold and hard crush it into little pieces.

If you feel up to it and working quickly but in a controlled fashion drizzle caramel patterns onto the greased baking tray and when cold lift gently and use to garnish ice creams.

Do be careful with recipes containing crushed caramel unless you fancy rather an evil kind of laugh. Shards of caramel do look and feel like broken glass. I have had some very satisfying complaints from customers which turned into profuse apologies as the thing they were so angry about melted deliciously in their mouths. A possible way around this problem might be to make these ice creams well in advance as I have been led to believe that crushed caramel folded into ice cream will eventually soften into pockets and ripples of gooey, um … ripples. Who knows?

Roasted/Toasted Nuts & Seeds

Roasting or toasting nuts and seeds makes them crunchy and fragrant – spread them on a baking tray and bake for 5-10 minutes in a medium oven (180°C/350°F/160°C fan/gas 4 ish) till they have darkened slightly and smell good Keep an eye on them whilst cooking and stir once or twice. Or get a similar result by tossing and stirring in a dry frying pan over medium heat. Cool before using. Store in an airtight container.

Praline and Brittle

Set 90g/⅔ cup of seeds or chopped nuts (roasted or otherwise) beside the stove. Make caramel as above and when a rich golden-brown stir in the nuts and then immediately decant onto the greased baking tray. When cold crush to praline and fold into ice cream just before freezing or break into pretty nut brittle shards to garnish sundaes and so on.

Coffee Brittle

As above but substitute coarsely ground coffee beans for the nuts.

Bacon Brittle

The same yet again but adding crunchy cooked bacon to the caramel. This goes very well, as one would expect, with Maple Syrup Ice Cream – page 10.

How to Vastly Improve Desiccated Coconut

200g/1 cup sugar
60ml/¼ cup water
200g/2 cups desiccated coconut

~ Stir the sugar and water together over low heat till the sugar dissolves. Bring to a boil.
~ Add the desiccated coconut and stir all together – the coconut will absorb the syrup.
~ Spread the moist coconut in a shallow layer on a baking tray and set aside to dry which will take all day or overnight, depending when you do it. It can be stored in the fridge for several days or frozen at this stage.

Crunchy Crumble Topping

200g/1¾ cups plain flour
100g/1 stick cold butter or margarine
50g/¼ cup sugar

~ Combine the flour and butter till the mixture resembles breadcrumbs – you can do this in a food processor or rub in by hand.
~ Stir in the sugar.
~ Spread onto a baking tray and cook in a medium oven (say 190ºC/375ºF/170ºC fan/gas 5) for about 20 minutes, stirring once or twice, till crisp.
~ Cool, freeze and use straight from the freezer.

Chocolate Bark

~ Melt chosen chocolate in accordance with instructions on page 44.
~ Spread the mixture onto a greaseproof lined baking tray and sprinkle with chosen toppings which could be chopped nuts, toasted coconut, dried fruit, crystallised chilli, crumbled biscuits etc.
~ Cool completely.
~ Break into pieces to garnish ice cream desserts (and others).

Failproof Meringue ~ honestly!

I'm maybe tempting fate calling these meringues "failproof" but they have always worked for me and for everyone I have given the recipe to. However here are a few pointers ...

~ Get the eggs out of the fridge, if they are in there, an hour or two before using because they will whisk up better when not so cold. Also older eggs whites are better for meringues than new ones, if you have a choice.
~ Keep all grease utterly away from the egg whites or they will not whisk, this includes egg yolk, if there is any in the whites either remove it with a piece of shell or start again.
~ Whisk the whites till very thick, in fact the classic test is if you can turn the bowl upside down and the meringue doesn't move it's ready. I wouldn't try this unless you are fairly confident.

2 egg whites
340g/1¾ cups caster sugar
1 tsp pure vanilla extract
a drip or two of food colouring if you feel like it
3 tablespoons of boiling water

~ Preheat oven to 110°C/225°F/90°C fan/gas ¼.
~ Line a baking tray with lightly greased greaseproof paper or parchment.
~ Start whisking together the egg whites, sugar and vanilla and then, whilst whisking, add the boiling water and food colouring if using.
~ Continue to whisk on high speed till the meringue is thick and stands in peaks.
~ Spoon or pipe the meringue into small dollops or pretty shapes onto the trays.
~ Bake for about 90 minutes till the meringues are crisp and dry.
~ Gently lift the meringues onto a cooling rack and cool completely.
~ Store in an airtight container for up to 2 weeks.

This makes about twelve 5cm/2" meringues.

Brown Sugar Meringues

A pleasing variation is to use brown sugar in the recipe – replace half the caster sugar with soft dark brown sugar.

Coffee Meringues

These are good too. Dissolve four teaspoons of instant coffee granules in the hot water before adding to the egg whites or use 50ml/3 tablespoons of double strength freshly brewed coffee. For a more intense effect also whip in 2 tablespoons of ground coffee.

Pink Peppercorn Meringues

Fold in a tablespoon of crushed pink peppercorns – these are particularly pretty and tasty with strawberries.

Squidgy Chocolate Meringues

These are glorious, I advise you not to leave them lying around in public – they really are most enticing

180g/1½ cups coarsely chopped dark chocolate
2 large room temperature egg whites
½ teaspoon cream of tartar
½ teaspoon pure vanilla extract
50g/¼ cup caster sugar

~ Melt the chocolate in accordance with the instructions on page 44.
~ Cool a little but it should still be runny.
~ Preheat your oven to 180°C/350°F/160°C fan/gas 4 and line a baking tray with baking parchment or a non-stick liner.
~ Whisk the egg whites together with the cream of tartar (abiding by the same meringue rules as above) to soft peaks.
~ Add the vanilla extract and then, still whisking, gradually add the sugar and whisk to stiff peaks.

~ Add the cooled chocolate and fold in gently, gently till all merged together.
~ Immediately drop teaspoonfully onto the parchment a couple of centimetres apart and bake till shiny and cracked – about 15-20 minutes.
~ Cool still on the tray on a cooling rack.

Either fold these darlings into an ice cream or eat quite soon (not difficult) although they will do fine for 2 or 3 days in an airtight container. This recipe makes about 20 so you could do both.

If, inexplicably, you have no ice cream, fill these meringues with whipped or, even better, clotted cream.

Tuiles

This is a handy recipe as the batter, which must be chilled for a few hours before use, can actually be kept in the fridge for up to a week before using. Also the resulting tuiles remain crisp for… well I don't know how long. I kept a few of my first batch in a fairly large box (so lots of air) and tried a bit every day (whilst relaxing with a coffee – this writing lark's exhausting!) and they never lost their lovely crispness over a week or more when suddenly … they were all gone!

Add a drop of food colouring and or a little extra flavour (citrus zest, cinnamon or coffee powder for instance) to the basic recipe if you wish.

4 egg whites
130g/⅔ cup granulated sugar
160g/⅔ cup butter - melted and cooled but still liquid
90g/¾ cup plain flour
pinch salt
scant teaspoon of vanilla extract

~ Whisk together the egg whites and the sugar to just mixed – don't keep whisking and accidentally make meringue!
~ Whisk in the melted butter.
~ Whisk in the flour and the salt.
~ Whisk in the vanilla extract and continue whisking till completely smooth.
~ Press and piece of cling film or similar onto the complete surface of the batter, cover and keep in the fridge for at least 4 hours.

To bake …

Don't cook many at once as they must be shaped as soon as they leave the oven, although if they do become too crisp to work put them back in for a minute or so to soften and try again.

~ Preheat the oven to 180°C/350°F/160°C fan/gas 4.
~ Use a very flat baking tray, line with greaseproof paper, parchment or, even better, a non-stick liner and grease it lightly.
~ Take a teaspoon or two of batter and spread as thinly as possible into a circle (or whatever shape you fancy).
~ Bake till the edges are golden brown and the middle looks dry and cooked, this takes about 10 minutes but watch carefully.
~ Have ready any shaping tool you have in mind.
~ As soon as the tuile is out of the oven slide a thin spatula under an edge and carefully lift/slide it off the tray and either cool on a rack or mould as required.

Ideas for shaping tuiles …

~ Drape over inverted ramekins, cups or similar to cool into little bowls.
~ Roll into cones either freeform or using a mould.
~ Roll round wooden spoon handles to make "cigars" or tubes.
~ Bake long, thin tuiles and corkscrew around wooden spoon handles.
~ Cool flat and layer up with ice cream.
~ Lay a few wooden spoon handles on a cooling rack and then drape with warm tuiles helping them to drop between the handles so that they go all wiggly!
~ If you are of an artistic bent or have the special templates available bake tuile spoons, hands, butterflies, flowers etc.

Brandy Snaps

This is a very simple. easy to remember recipe, just equal quantities of each major ingredient – butter, sugar, Golden Syrup and flour - plus a little flavouring in the form of ground ginger, perhaps cinnamon or lemon zest and, of course, brandy. I say "of course" but a surprisingly large number of brandy snaps contain no brandy. Not mine though, even if it is just a token gesture

Moulding - don't bake too many brandy snaps at a time as you need to work quickly to shape them once they are out of the oven, alternating baking trays is a good idea. See Tuiles above for shaping ideas. The following quantities makes about six x 10cm/4" baskets.

60g/½ stick butter
50g/¼ cup granulated or caster sugar
2 tablespoons Golden Syrup
60g/½ cup plain flour
½ teaspoon ground ginger
1 teaspoon brandy

~ Preheat oven to 180°C/350°F/160°C fan/ gas 4.
~ In a small pan melt together the first three ingredients over medium heat, stirring till smooth.
~ Allow to cool for a few minutes then stir in the rest of the ingredients.
~ Lightly grease a baking tray or two and spoon one or two brandy snaps onto each tray. Spread thinly in a round (to make baskets), or a strip (to make twirls) or any other shape you feel inspired to create. Leave plenty of space as they spread.
~ Bake till the batter has spread and bubbled and become a dark golden lace on the baking tray – about 10 minutes. Remove from the oven and allow to sit a few minutes till you can manipulate the brandy snap off the tray and onto or around your mould. See Tuiles above for some ideas in this regard.
~ Cool completely in situ and then keep in an airtight container but not for too long. If they do soften return to a medium oven for a few minutes, re-shape and re-cool.

Broken bits are good just sprinkled over ice cream.

Cones

This recipe which is somewhat akin to pancakes, or crêpes, is the first cone recipe I tried because it is cooked on the stove top rather than in the oven. If you met my oven you'd understand. The resulting cones are not only convenient they are also delicious, so I didn't try any other recipes (see photo on page 43 for one in use)!

2 eggs
100g/½ cup caster sugar
60g/½ stick butter – melted
2 tablespoon milk
2-3 drips of vanilla extract
50g/⅓ cup plain flour
pinch salt

~ Beat together the eggs and the sugar till thick then beat in the melted butter, the milk and the vanilla.
~ Whisk in the flour and salt and if necessary add a little more milk to make a

smooth and runny batter the consistency of single cream.
- ~ Lightly oil a 24cm/9" non-stick pan and put over medium heat.
- ~ Pour in about 60ml/¼ cup of the batter and tip and rotate the pan to form a thin round pancake.
- ~ Cook over medium heat till the edges and underneath are golden.
- ~ Carefully turn and cook the other side till this too is golden.
- ~ Turn out on a flat surface and immediately, roll into a cornet – making a card cone first can help with this.
- ~ Set aside on a rack whilst making the rest of the cones – they will crisp as they cool.
- ~ Repeat till all the batter is gone.

Use the cones within the next couple of hours or, if you can't, re-warm slightly in a medium hot oven to pliable, re-roll and re-cool.

~ *Sexy Ideas & Presentations* ~

Ice creams can be served in all sorts of ice cream enhancing and amusing ways, some of which are already mentioned above in previous chapters. The easiest way to make ice cream attractive (as if it needs help!) is to serve in pretty shapes or containers but here are some other ideas that might be of use.

Sundae Sermon

The ice cream sundae, or at least the name "sundae", originated in America, although apparently there is much discussion as to which bit of America. Sundaes were invented when it became illegal to sell ice-cream sodas on a Sunday in the town of Evanston, or somewhere else, during the late 19th century. To get around the problem some traders replaced the soda with syrup and the final "y" with an "e" to avoid upsetting religious types.

In England we have the traditional sundae-like Knickerbocker Glory which is layers of fruit, jelly and cream served in a tall glass. In America a Knickerbocker Glory sort of thing is known as a Parfait although this word is French for perfect, which perhaps it is to them. In France (and to me) parfait generally means a kind of frozen mousse using hot syrup or meringue to make the ice cream. I'm glad I managed to clear that up for you.

Generally speaking a sundae is a dish, often a pretty glass dish, of ice cream with complimentary fruits, nuts, sauces, etc. Here are a few ideas …

~ Banoffee Crunch Sundae – Rum Roasted Banana Ice Cream (page 33), Sticky Toffee Sauce (page 79), and crushed digestive biscuits which have been sautéed for a few minutes in a little butter.
~ Cranachan – toast a handful of porridge oats in a dry frying pan together with light brown sugar. Cool and layer with Raspberry Ice Cream (page 27), Honey Ice Cream (page 10) and fresh raspberries tossed in a wee nip of whisky. Tall glass, layers, top layer oatmeal, whipped cream with a perfect raspberry perching on top.
~ Black Forest Sundae – Brandied Cherry and White Chocolate Ice Cream (page 50), Dark Chocolate Ice Cream (page 44), chocolate shavings and bits of chocolate cake soaked in Kirsch.
~ Poire Belle Helène Sundae – a chocolate ice cream of your choice, Butterscotch Baked Pear Ice Cream (page 34), chocolate sauce and whipped cream.
~ Honey Nut Sundae - honey ice cream (page 10), honey roast nuts, runny honey and cream – salted peanuts are good in this too.

Affogato

… is Italian for "drowned" and in the foodie world usually refers to ice cream "drowned" in espresso, in which case its full name is Affogato al Caffe.

In experimentation for this book I have, repeatedly I'm afraid, made a delicious Affogato by pouring some good strong coffee (remember I live in a caravan and a boat so espresso itself is not that easy to achieve), spiked with a little brandy, over my homemade Double Vanilla Ice Cream (page 19) and then, a touch of genius, I crumble an Amaretti or other biccie over the dish. I love it and it is so easy and spontaneous provided you have ice cream in the freezer and, as you have got this far in the book, I am assuming you have. If you are serving this at a dinner party or such it might be an idea to serve the ice cream with the coffee in a little jug on the side so that guests can drown their own ice cream and get the full hot coffee/cold ice cream effect. You can, however, drown any ice cream you like in any sort of coffee or even some other drinkable liquid, I suppose. Maybe a Mocha Affogato with chocolate ice cream or maybe White Chocolate Chip Ice Cream (page 47), coffee, Tia Maria and grated dark chocolate or how about Lemon Posset Ice Cream (page 25), Limoncello and Crystallised Orange (page 88)?

As this is a cross between a sundae and a beverage I toyed with putting it in the drinks section but being easiest eaten with a spoon I decided on this location.

Per person …

1 scoop chosen ice cream
1 shot/2 tablespoons espresso or strong coffee or whatever your choice is
1 tablespoon brandy or some other spirit or liqueur - optional
2 amaretti or something suitable and crumbly – optional

~ Chill serving dish(es).
~ Put a scoop of chosen ice cream into each dish and return to the freezer for a few minutes.
~ Brew coffee or espresso.
~ Have ready chosen liqueur if using.
~ Crumble crumbly thing if using.
~ Remove ice cream from freezer and swiftly and immediately pour liqueur and coffee over it.
~ Sprinkle with crumbly thing and serve.

Leading on from Affogato and in a slightly similar vein …

Coffee Ice Cream melting in a Bittersweet Chocolate Soup

I am a great believer in the power of words. This is of course, just ice cream with hot chocolate sauce, cunningly disguised. The first time I put it on a menu it sold like nobody's business and people asked, in awe and wonder, whence I got such a marvellous recipe

Coconut Ice Ice (Baby)

500ml/2 cups double cream
200g/⅔ cup condensed milk
80ml/⅓ cup vanilla syrup
1 batch of vastly improved desiccated coconut – page 93
a few drops of red food colouring

~ Whisk the cream till thick.
~ Fold in the condensed milk together with the coconut and the vanilla syrup.
~ Spread half into a shallow square freezer proof dish to a depth of about 1 cm/½".
~ Add a drip or two of food colouring to the other half and fold in till uniformly pink and pretty, add a little more if necessary but a little goes a very long way.
~ Carefully spread this over the first white half of the ice cream without disturbing it.
~ Freeze.
~ Cut into cubes and serve in a pretty girly sort of a way.

Ice Cream Truffles

This is a good way to use up bits of leftover ice cream – something that happens to me a lot – and impress people at the same time. Scoop ice cream into small balls and coat in something complimentary such as cocoa, crushed biscuits, ground caramel, chopped nuts, sprinkles, grated chocolate and so on.

Profiteroles

I used to have a husband that called these "poovy boirays" – no idea why, bless him. They are little choux pastry puffs filled with cream and often drizzled with chocolate and are well worth eating. Replace the cream filling with ice cream and drizzle the tops with a complimentary sauce.

Terrines

I always freeze terrines in silicone loaf "pans", they turn out so neatly. An advantage of serving ice cream this way is that, if it is a little on the firm side, it will slice neatly and then soften quite quickly on the plate. Remember that the bottom of the container will be the top of the terrine so put any decoration in first. Layer up contrasts in both colour and flavour, for instance …

~ Coffee (page 17), Dark Chocolate (page 44) and Double Vanilla (page 19) or one of the Banana (page 33) ice creams.
~ Mango-Lime (page 35), Toasted Coconut (page 39) and Painkiller (page 53) ice creams.
~ Blue Cheese (page 72), Butterscotch Baked Pear (page 34) and Black Pepper (page 70) ices creams.
~ Maple Syrup (page 10) with Pecan Praline (page 38) or Butternut Bourbon (page 38).
~ Crunchy Peanut Butter (page 13) and Jam (page 14) ice creams sprinkled with crushed Bacon Brittle (page 92)!

Bombes

Similar to a terrine in concept but a different shape. Spread softened ice cream into a bowl mould; using the back of a spoon is easiest I find. Freeze this layer till good and solid and repeat with the next batch of softened ice cream. Continue till your bowl is full and your patience has run out using complimentary flavours and freezing between each layer. Turn out and cut into wedges to serve.

… *Sexy Ideas & Presentations* …

Fruit Shells

This is a food fashion from the early 80's; serving ice cream in the skin of its relevant fruit. Now it is no longer so common I don't mind doing it myself on occasion. Just cut the fruit (probably citrus is best) in half across its equator, remove all the flesh and make ice cream with it. Pile the ice cream into the empty fruit halves and freeze. You might have to cut a sliver off the bottom of the fruit shells, so they don't roll off the plate

2 Hot Ice Cream Dishes

Very lush soft ice creams are not suitable for these two dishes; use something on the firmer side.

Baked Alaska

~ Top sponge cake or brownies, about 2.5cm/1" thick, with scoops of ice cream leaving an edge.
~ Drizzle the cake or the ice cream with a sauce if you wish.
~ Put in the freezer and leave there till well 'ard!
~ Preheat oven 230°C/450°F/210°C fan/gas 8.
~ Starting at the base and working quickly cover completely with meringue (the recipe is on page 94) leaving no hint of a gap.
~ Without delay put it into the oven for just three or four minutes till the meringue is touched with gold.
~ Serve absolutely immediately.

Ice Cream Fritters

~ Scoop ice cream into nicely formed balls and return to the freezer till very firm.
~ Crush a packet of digestive biscuits and roll the ice cream balls in half the crumbs to coat. Re-freeze.
~ Beat an egg or two and, working very quickly, dip the frozen balls into the egg and then into the other half of the biscuit crumbs to form an unbroken coat. Return to the freezer yet again for an hour or more.

~ Deep fry in clean hot oil (190 °C/375 °F) for just 10 or 12 seconds or so till golden and serve pronto.

Ice Cream Cakes

Shortly before serving use a softened complimentary ice cream to fill and top a cake and pop back into the freezer for a few minutes for the ice cream to firm up. Slice and serve.

Ice Cream Tarts

An easily splendid way to present ice cream is in the form of a tart. Pile or layer up complimentary flavours in cool, pre-baked pastry or biscuit crusts. Here are just a few ideas to get you started …

~ Apple Crumble – fill the case with Toffee Apple Ice Cream (page 31) or Bramley Apple and Cider Ice Cream (page 52) and sprinkle with Crunchy Crumble Topping (page 93).
~ Banana Split Pie – start with a layer of sliced fresh bananas and top with one of the banana ice creams (page 33). Freeze and serve drizzled with not one but two sauces! – Extreme Chocolate Sauce (page 78) and also Sticky Toffee Sauce (page 78). Add whipped cream and toasted nuts too. Go wild!
~ Pumpkin Pie – use the Butternut Squash and Maple Syrup Ice Cream on page 74 and sprinkle with toasted pecans or Pecan Praline (page 92).
~ Brandied Mincemeat Ice Cream Pie (see page 15 for the ice cream) decorated with baked pastry holly leaves.

Ice Cream Sandwiches

You'll be pleased I've put this info here because if you google "ice cream sandwich" it's all about Android! Basically just sandwich together two cookies or similar with ice cream and then either eat immediately or freeze and eat later. However to make things even better …

~ Choose your biscuit or cookie carefully – very crisp and crumbly is good as is soft and cakey as these will both be edible from the freezer. Chewy biscuits could freeze too hard. Or try thinly sliced brownies, brandy snaps, meringues or macaroons.
~ If purpose baking cookies slightly undercook to keep the texture right when frozen, and …

~ … sandwich whilst still warm with very cold ice cream which will slightly melt and soak into the cookie before setting solid in the freezer – even more goo-some!
~ Fill generously, make a neat edge and you could roll it in chopped chocolate, nuts or sprinkles.

Ginger biscuits with Lemon Posset Ice Cream (page 22) are some of the best IMHO and oaty biscuits with Honey Ice Cream are good too! These are almond cookies with Brandied Cherry and White Chocolate Ice Cream (page 50).

Cones, Cornets & Pokes!

So far as I can ascertain these are all the same thing; poke being a Northern Irish term. I used to frequent a gorgeous tropical garden eatery in the Virgin Islands called The Garden of Luscious Licks where, of course, excellent ice creams were on the menu. I always think of that place when licking an ice cream cone.

Obviously, directions for assembling ice cream cones aren't really necessary but I do have a few things to say.

~ Idea – put a delicious little something into the point of the cone to stop any leakages. Choose something complimentary to your chosen ice cream such as peanut butter, melted choc, caramel, a bit of marshmallow, etc.
~ Suggestion – make your own "Cornetto"; fill the entire cone with ice cream and level the surface. Spread the top (and the sides if you fancy it) with melted chocolate, sprinkle with nuts and re-freeze.
~ Reminder – as I am sure you know it is illegal to have an ice cream cone in your pocket when in Lexington, Kentucky in case you upset a horse.

Milk Shakes

Easy peasy - liquidise together approximately twice as much ice cream as milk to make a pleasantly drinkable concoction, together with fruits or syrup or sauce to taste. You could even add a little spirit or liqueur for an Adult Milkshake.

Ice Cream Soda or Float aka a Spider in Australia!

The method is thus …

~ Put a spoonful or two of your chosen sauce or syrup into a tall glass.
~ Loosen it with a splash of your chosen soda.
~ Stir in a spoonful or two of milk or cream.
~ Add a couple of scoops of your chosen ice cream.
~ Top up with more of your chosen soda; hopefully the mixture should fizz and froth delightfully.
~ Top with whipped cream and your chosen decoration be it a flake, sprinkle or a cherry on top.
~ Serve with both a straw and a long spoon.

As you can see there is a lot of choosing involved. Here are a few ideas that may, or in some cases may not, help:

~ Root Beer Float –to me Root Beer tastes like Deep Heat so I can't recommend it. If you do have a go use vanilla (page 19) or chocolate ice cream (page 44) and maybe a chocolate sauce (page 78). This is also known as a Brown Cow.
~ Different colour cows can be achieved with different sodas – for instance a Purple Cow with Grape Soda or a Pink Cow with Cherry Soda.
~ Irn Bru – as this is made with girders perhaps it could be a good alternative to root beer in the UK. Again, I'd go for vanilla ice cream (page 19).

~ Coca Cola Float – as above again but possibly nicer! These are also sometimes called Brown Cows.

Now that's got the "classics" out the way how about the following?

~ Lemon or Orange Ice Cream (page 15) with Lemon or Orange Soda
~ Chocolate Ice Cream (page 44) with Ginger Beer
~ Toffee Apple Ice Cream (page 31) with Cider
~ Banana Ice Cream (page 33) with Cream Soda
~ Marzipan Ice Cream (page 40) and Cherry Soda
~ Peaches and Cream Ice Cream (page 28), a touch of Peach Schnapps (eg. Archers) with Cream Soda. Which leads me on to …

Ice Cream Cocktails

Basically blend together complimentary liqueurs, fruits, sauces and ice cream and give it a suggestive name such as Lose Your Cherry (cherry brandy, Vanilla Ice Cream, page 19, and cream soda) or Fuzzy Navel (Peaches and Cream Ice Cream, page 28, Peach Schnapps and Orange Juice). Other suggestions, for 2 people, include …

~ White Russian – 250ml/1 cup Vanilla Ice Cream (page 29) together with 60ml/¼ cup each (yes) of vodka and Kahlua. Garish with chocolate shavings.
~ BBC – 250ml/1 cup Rum Roasted Banana Ice Cream (page 33), 60m/¼ cup each dark rum and Baileys, maybe a fresh banana if you have one.
~ Fruit Punch – 250ml/1 cup Mango-Lime Ice Cream (page 35) and 60ml/¼ cup each golden rum and Malibu. Sprinkle with toasted coconut.
~ Mudslide – 250ml/1 cup Double Vanilla Ice Cream (page 19), 3 tablespoon each vodka, Kahlua and Baileys plus chocky sauce to taste.
~ Mojito – Fresh Mint Ice Cream (page 41), good sloosh of golden rum and top up with soda water. Garnish with a sprig of mint.

Cheers!

~ *Summing up and Endnotes* ~

That's about all I can think of to tell you.

Now you have a go!

I'd like to thank Paul for licking the bowls although, on rare occasions, I have licked them myself whilst assuming a thoughtful researcher-ish demeanour.

I'd also like to thank you so much for reading this, I really hope you enjoyed it and all the ice creams you make.

Good reviews are important to a book's success helping others to find good reading. If enjoyed this book (or indeed any book by anyone) please take the time to review it on Amazon. Just a few lines will be a real help and I'll be very grateful!

Suzy Bowler

~ Index ~

Alcohol …

    Alcoholic by Necessity Trifle Ice Cream   65
    Amaretti Amaretto Ice Cream   52
    Apple Cider Sauce   80
    Baileys Ice Cream   55
    Blue Cheese & Port Ripple   74
    Bramley Apple and Cider Ice Cream   52
    Brandied Cherry and White Chocolate Ice Cream   50
    Brandied Mincemeat Ice Cream   15
    Buttered Nut & Bourbon Ice Cream   38
    Buttered Rum & Ginger Ice Cream   55
    Caramel/Pineapple/Rum Sauce   80
    Honey Mead Ice Cream   56
    Ice Cream Cocktails   109
    Neat Spirit and Liqueur Ice Creams   56
    Painkiller Ice Cream   53
    Port and Orange Ice Cream   33
    Port Syrup   88
    Prune & Armagnac   51
    Rum & Raisin Ice Cream   51
    Rum Roasted Banana Ice Cream   33
    Red Wine Syrup   88
    Spirit & Liqueur Syrups   87
    'Ti Punch Ice Cream   54

Affogato   102

Amaretti Amaretto Ice Cream   52

Apple …

    Apple Cider Sauce   80
    Bramley Apple and Cider Ice Cream   52
    Toffee Apple Ice Cream   31

Bacon …

    Bacon & Maple Syrup Ice Cream   72
    Bacon Brittle   92

Baileys Ice Cream   55

Baked Alaska   105

Banana …

    Banana Fudge Ice Cream   33
    Banana Rum Cake Ice Cream   68
    Rum Roasted Banana Ice Cream   33

Beetroot and Chocolate Ice Cream   76

Black Garlic Ice Cream   76

Black Pepper Ice Cream   70

Black Pepper Syrup   85

Blackberry Ice Cream   30

Blueberry Fool Ice   28

Bombes   104

Bourbon …

    Bourbon Syrup   87
    Butternut & Bourbon Ice Cream   38

Brain Freeze   8

Brandy …

    Brandied Cherry & White Chocolate Ice Cream   50
    Brandied Mincemeat Ice Cream   15
    Brandy Snaps   97
    Brandy Syrup   87

Brittle …

    Bacon Brittle   92
    Coffee Brittle   92
    Nut Brittle   92

Brown Bread Ice Cream   60

Brown Sugar …

    Brown Sugar Ice Cream   25
    Brown Sugar Meringues   95
    Peach and Brown Sugar Meringue Ice Cream   62
    Sautéed Peach and Brown Sugar Ice Cream   31

Buttered Nut & Bourbon Ice Cream   38

Butternut Squash (or Pumpkin) & Maple Syrup Ice Cream   75

Butterscotch Baked Pear Ice Cream   34

Cakes   106

Caramel …

    Caramel Ice Cream   24
    Caramelised Cinnamon Ice Cream   24
    Caramel/Pineapple/Rum Sauce   80
    Caramel Syrup   86
    Chocolate Brownie Caramel Swirl   63
    Chocolate Caramel Sauce   79
    How to Make Caramel   91
    Salted Caramel Crunch   24

Carrot Cake Ice Cream   67

Cheese …

    Blue Cheese & Baked Pear Ice Cream   73
    Blue Cheese & Port Ripple   73
    Blue Cheese Ice Cream   72
    Goats Cheese and Hazelnut Ice Cream   74
    Peppered Blue Cheese Ice Cream   74
    Peppered Goat Cheese Ice Cream   75

Cherry …

    Brandied Cherry & White Chocolate Ice Cream   50

Chilli …

Chilli Syrup 89
Chocolate-Chilli Ripple 47
Crystallised Chilli 89

Chocolate …

    Brandied Cherry and White Chocolate Ice Cream 50
    Chewy Double Chocolate Ice Cream 48
    Chocolate and Crunchy Peanut Butter Ripple 45
    Chocolate and Peanut Butter Swirl 13
    Chocolate Bark 93
    Chocolate Brownie Caramel Swirl 63
    Chocolate Caramel Sauces 79
    Chocolate Caramel Semifreddo-ish 45
    Chocolate-Chilli Ripple 47
    Chocolate Ginger Crunch 60
    Chocolate Meringues 95
    Cocoa Nib Ice Cream 23
    Coffee, Kahlua and Chocolate Meringue Ice Cream 62
    Dark Chocolate and Candied Orange Ice Cream 46
    Dark Chocolate Ice Cream 44
    Extreme Chocolate Sauce 78
    How to Melt Chocolate 44
    Roasted Beetroot & Chocolate Ice Cream 76
    Rocky Road 78
    Sticky Chocolate Sauce 78
    Stracciatella Ice Cream 63
    Über Mocha 46

    White Chocolate & Coffee Ice Cream 48
    White Chocolate Chip Ice Cream 47

Christmas Pudding Ice Cream 66

Cider …

    Apple and Cider Ice Cream 52
    Apple Cider Sauce 80

Cinnamon …

    Caramelised Cinnamon Ice Cream 24
    Cinnamon Toast Ice Cream 61

Clotted Cream Ice Cream 4

Cocoa Nib Ice Cream 23

Cocktails 109

Coconut …

    Coconut Ice Ice 103
    How to Improve Desiccated Coconut 93
    Painkiller Ice Cream 53
    Toasted Coconut Ice Cream 39

Coffee …

    Affogato 102
    Coffee and White Chocolate Ice Cream 48
    Coffee Brittle 92
    Coffee Ice Cream 17
    Coffee, Kahlua & Chocolate Meringue Ice Cream 62
    Coffee Meringues 95

Coffee Syrup   87
Elevensies Ice Cream   59
Über Mocha   46

Cones/Cornets …

    Cones Recipe   98
    Cornets, assembling   107

Crumble Topping   93

Drinks …

    Affogato   102
    Ice Cream Cocktail   109
    Ice Cream Sodas   108
    Milk Shakes   107

Dulce de Leche …

    Dulce de Leche Ice Cream   6
    Dulce de Leche Ripple   12
    How to Make Dulce de Leche   6

Elderflower Ice Cream   17

Elevensies Ice Cream   59

Figs, Honey Roasted, Ice Cream   34

Folding In   5

Freezing directions   7

Fritters   105

Fruit …

    Coulis & Sauces   82
    Crystallised   83
    Shells   105

Fudge Crumble Ice Cream   64

GENIUS RECIPE   3

Ginger …

    Buttered Rum & Ginger Ice Cream   55
    Chocolate Ginger Crunch   60
    Ginger Syrup   85
    Honey and Ginger Ice Cream   10
    Jamaican Gingerbread Ice Cream   68
    Papaya and Ginger Ice Cream   29

Golden Syrup …

    Thunder & Lightening Ice   12
    Treacle Pudding Ice Cream   67

Greek Yogurt and Honey Ice Cream   12

Herbs …

    Lavender Honey Ice Cream   11
    Lavender Ice Cream   42
    Lavender Syrup   86
    Mint Ice Cream   41

Honey …

    Greek Yogurt & Honey Ice   12
    Honey & Ginger Ice Cream   10
    Honey & Lemon Ice Cream   11
    Honey Ice Cream   10
    Honey Mead Ice Cream   56
    Honey Roasted Fig Ice Cream   34

Lavender Honey Ice Cream   11

Honeycomb Ice Cream   64

Hot Cross Bun Ice Cream   61

Hot Ice Cream Dishes …

    Baked Alaska   105
    Ice Cream Fritters   105

Ice Cream Headache   8

Inclusions, how to add them   6

Island Spice Ice Cream   20

Jamaican Gingerbread Ice Cream   68

Jam Ice Cream   14

Lavender …

    Lavender Honey Ice Cream   11
    Lavender Ice Cream   42
    Lavender Syrup   86

Lemon …

    Honey & Lemon Ice Cream   11
    Lemon Curd   88
    Lemon Curd Ice Cream   15
    Lemon Meringue Ice Cream   22
    Lemon Posset Ice Cream   22
    St. Clement's Ice Cream   22

Lime …

    Lime Curd   81
    Lime Curd Ice Cream   15
    Mango Lime Ice Cream   35

Liquorice …

    Liquorice Ice Cream   21
    Salty Liquorice Ice Cream   21

Mango Lime Ice Cream   35

Maple Syrup …

    Maple Syrup and Bacon Ice Cream   72
    Maple Syrup & Butternut Squash (or Pumpkin) Ice Cream   75
    Maple Syrup Ice Cream   10

Marbling   5

Marmalade Ice Cream   14

Marzipan Ice Cream   40

Meringues …

    Brown Sugar Meringues   95
    Chocolate Meringues   95
    Coffee, Kahlua & Chocolate Meringue Ice Cream   62
    Coffee Meringues   95
    Eton Mess Ice Cream   62
    Failproof Meringues   94
    Peach and Brown Sugar Meringue Ice Cream   62
    Pink Peppercorn Meringues   95

Milk Shakes   107

Mint Ice Cream   41

Nutella Fudge Ripple   16

Nuts …

    Buttered Nut & Bourbon Ice
      Cream   38
    Chocolate and Crunchy Peanut
      Butter Ripple   45
    Crunchy Peanut Butter Ice
      Cream   13
    Goat Cheese & Hazelnut Ice
      Cream   74
    Marzipan Ice Cream   40
    Nut Brittle   92
    Nutella Fudge Ripple   16
    Peanut Butter & Chocolate
      Swirl   13
    P.B. & J.I.C.   13
    Praline   92
    Praline Ice Cream   38
    Roasted/Toasted Nuts   92
    Salt and Pepper Cashew
      Brittle   39

Orange …

    Boodle-ish Orange Fool Ice
      Cream   65
    Burnt Orange Ice Cream   32
    Crystallised Orange and its
      Ensuing Syrup   100
    Dark Chocolate and Candied
      Orange Ice Cream   46
    Orange Curd   81
    Orange Curd Ice Cream   15
    Port and Orange Ice Cream   33
    St. Clement's Ice Cream   22

Painkiller Ice Cream   53

Papaya and Ginger Ice Cream   29

Peaches …

    Peach and Brown Sugar
      Meringue Ice Cream   62
    Peaches and Cream Ice
      Cream   28
    Peach Melba Ripple   29
    Sautéed Peach & Brown
      Sugar Ice Cream   31

Peanut Butter …

    Chocolate and Crunchy Peanut
      Butter Ripple   45
    Crunchy Peanut Butter Ice
      Cream   13
    P.B. & J.I.C.   13
    Peanut Butter and Chocolate
      Swirl   13

Pear …

    Blue Cheese and Baked Pear Ice
      Cream   73
    Butterscotch Baked Pear Ice
      Cream   34

Pepper …

    Black Pepper Ice Cream   70
    Black Pepper Syrup   85
    Peppered Blue Cheese Ice
      Cream   74
    Peppered Goats Cheese Ice
      Cream   75
    Pink Peppercorn Meringues   95

Pineapple …

   Caramel/Pineapple/Rum
    Sauce 80
   Slow Roasted Pineapple Ice
    Cream 35

Popping Candy Ice Cream 71

Port …

   Port and Blue Cheese Ice
    Cream 74
   Port and Orange Ice Cream 33
   Port Syrup 88

Praline …

   Praline 92
   Praline Ice Cream 38

Profiteroles 104

Prune & Armagnac Ice Cream 51

Pumpkin & Maple Syrup Ice Cream 75

Raspberry …

   Peach Melba Ice Cream 29
   Raspberry Curd 81
   Raspberry Curd Ice Cream 15
   Raspberry Ripple 27

Red Wine Syrup 88

Rhubarb Ice Cream 30
Rocky Road 58

Rum …

   Banana Rum Cake Ice Cream 68
   Buttered Rum & Ginger Ice
    Cream 55
   Caramel/Pineapple/Rum
    Sauce 80
   Painkiller Ice Cream 58
   Pina Colada Ice Cream 58
   Rum & Raisin Ice Cream 51
   Rum Roasted Banana Ice
    Cream 33
   Rum Syrup 87
   'Ti Punch Ice Cream 54

Salt …

   Salt and Pepper Cashew
    Brittle 39
   Salted Caramel Crunch 24
   Salty Liquorice Ice Cream 21

Sandwiches 106

Sauces …

   Apple Cider Sauce 80
   Caramel/Pineapple/Rum
    Sauce 80
   Chocolate Caramel Sauces 79
   Extreme Chocolate Sauce 78
   Fresh Fruit Sauces 82
   Sticky Chocolate Sauce 78
   Sticky Toffee Sauce 79

Sesame, Toasted, Ice Cream 39

Shelf Life 7
Sodas and Floats 108

Sticky Toffee Sauce 79

Stracciatella 63

Strawberry …

    Strawberry Balsamic Ripple   70
    Strawberry Ice Cream   27

Sundaes   101

Syrup … 83

    Basic Syrup Recipe   84
    Black Pepper Syrup   85
    Caramel Syrup   86
    Chilli Syrup   89
    Coffee Syrup   87
    Ginger Syrup   85
    Lavender Syrup   86
    Orange Syrup   88
    Port Syrup   88
    Red Wine Syrup   88
    Spirit Syrups   87
    Vanilla Syrup   86

Tarts   106

Terrines   104

Thunder & Lightening Ice Cream   12

'Ti Punch Ice Cream   54

Toffee …

    Sticky Toffee Pudding Ice Cream   68
    Sticky Toffee Sauce   79
    Toffee Apple Ice Cream   31
    Toffee Ripple   16

Treacle Pudding Ice Cream   67

Trifle Ice Cream, Alcoholic   65

Truffles   103

Tuiles   96

Tutti Frutti   58

Vanilla …

    Double Vanilla Ice Cream   19
    Vanilla Syrup   85

Werther's Original Crunch Ice Cream   71

Whisky Syrup   87

White Chocolate …

    Brandied Cherry & White Chocolate Ice Cream   50
    Coffee and White Chocolate Ice Cream   48
    White Chocolate Chip Ice Cream   47

Yogurt …

    Greek Yogurt and Honey Ice Cream   12

Printed in Great Britain
by Amazon

82443492R00074